THE KETCHUP LOVER'S COOKBOOK

HarperCollins*Publishers*
1 London Bridge Street
London SE1 9GF

www.harpercollins.co.uk

HarperCollins*Publishers*
1st Floor, Watermarque Building, Ringsend Road
Dublin 4, Ireland

First published by HarperCollins*Publishers* 2021

10 9 8 7 6 5 4 3 2

© HarperCollins*Publishers* 2021

Photography by Sam Folan
Food styling by Katie Marshall
Props by Max Robinson

A catalogue record of this book is available from the British Library.

HB ISBN 978-0-00-849235-9

Printed and bound in Latvia

When using kitchen appliances, please always follow the manufacturer's instructions.

MIX
Paper from
responsible sources
FSC™ C007454

This book is produced from independently certified FSC™ paper
to ensure responsible forest management.

For more information visit: www.harpercollins.co.uk/green

THE
KETCHUP
LOVER'S
COOKBOOK

HarperCollins*Publishers*

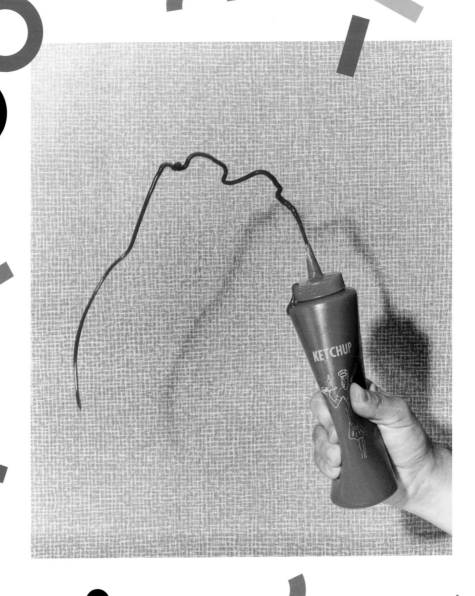

CONTENTS

INTRODUCTION

WHO DOESN'T LOVE KETCHUP? IT'S EVERYONE'S FAVOURITE CONDIMENT AND WE ALL HAVE AT LEAST ONE BOTTLE IN OUR KITCHEN CUPBOARDS. INDEED, IT'S ALMOST IMPOSSIBLE TO ENVISAGE EATING A BURGER, HOT DOG OR FRENCH FRIES WITHOUT IT. KETCHUP PLAYS AN INTRINSIC ROLE IN OUR GLOBAL FOOD CULTURE, TRANSCENDING DIFFERENCES IN TRADITIONAL AND NATIONAL CUISINES. IT HAS TRAVELLED WAY BEYOND THE BORDERS OF THE UNITED STATES, WHERE IT WAS FIRST MADE WITH TOMATOES, AND IS NOW CONSUMED ALL OVER THE WORLD.

HISTORY

The name 'ketchup' has its origins in China, where a spicy, dark pickled fish sauce was known as 'ke-tsiap'. From there it travelled to Vietnam, Indonesia and Malaysia where it was known as 'ketjap' or 'kechap'. British sailors brought it back to Europe in the seventeenth century and it soon became a popular spicy condiment, usually flavoured with mushrooms, walnuts or salty anchovies. Later, the early settlers took it across the Atlantic to America where the prototype of our familiar tomato ketchup was born. The first mention of a spicy tomato ketchup (or catsup) was found in a recipe dating from 1801, and soon it was being bottled commercially and sold as 'ketchup'.
The classic ketchup is made with ripe tomatoes, sugar, vinegar, salt and spices but this was not always the case. Until the 1906 Pure Food and Drugs Act, which banned the preservative sodium benzoate, in the United States, unripe green tomatoes were used in ketchup production and the consistency was much thinner.

Changing the traditional recipe to use ripe, red tomatoes for their colour, flavour and natural pectin (setting) content, as well as using vinegar and salt as preservatives instead of sodium benzoate, is how our beloved modern ketchup was born. The rest, as they say, is history.

TYPES OF KETCHUP

You can now buy ketchup everywhere and in a wide range of packaging – it's available in traditional glass bottles, squeezy plastic bottles, tubes and sachets. And it comes in a variety of flavours – low-sodium, reduced-sugar, honey-sweetened, hot ketchup, jalapeño and sriracha ketchup, and even ketchup with added vegetables. Organic alternatives are also common.

FLAVOUR AND NUTRITION

What makes ketchup so special is its unique flavour: sweet, slightly salty, tangy, spicy, sharp, mellow and piquant. Its magic lies in the fact that it can spice up even the blandest foods, making them more palatable, as well as enhancing crispy fried foods. This may be because it is one of the few foods that combines all five taste elements: salty, sweet, sour, bitter and umami. Many condiments and sauces only deliver at most two or three. The deep savoury umami quality of ketchup is probably what makes it so irresistible and universally liked.

And as well as having an awesome flavour, ketchup is nutritious, too. It's low in fat, and recent studies have shown that it can help to reduce 'bad' cholesterol (low-density lipoprotein). It's also a good source of vitamins A and C, which help to boost our immune system.

WHAT GOES WITH KETCHUP?

Almost anything savoury. You can serve ketchup for breakfast, brunch, lunch, dinner and snacks. As well as French fries, burgers, hot dogs, chicken nuggets and eggs, it's great with hash browns, French toast, toasted sandwiches, pies and grilled (broiled), barbecued and fried meat, poultry, fish and vegetables.

And you can use it as a flavouring ingredient as well as a condiment – even top chefs and Michelin-starred restaurants add ketchup to some of their dishes. In this book we have recipes for dips, marinades, sauces and salad dressings made with ketchup, including the classic seafood cocktail and barbecue sauces and glazes as well as Thousand Island dressing and a ketchup vinaigrette. Ketchup can add a tangy piquancy to Mexican nachos, burritos, quesadillas, pico de gallo (spicy salsa) and guacamole.

In the following pages, you will find Italian pasta sauces and pizza toppings enhanced with ketchup and salads with ketchup-spiked dressings, as well as soups, casseroles, Thai and Chinese suppers (pad Thai and even crispy duck with pancakes), Mediterranean baked fish and the great American favourites – meatloaf, baby back ribs, buffalo wings and Reuben sandwiches. There really is something for everyone.

Vegetarians and vegans can enjoy cooking with ketchup, too, whether it's a TLT sandwich (tofu, lettuce and tomato), jackfruit carnitas or refried bean tacos. And we have delicious comfort food, including ketchup mac 'n' cheese, a vegetarian shepherd's pie and clam chowder, to warm you up and lift your spirits. And if you want to be really adventurous and take your devotion to ketchup one step further, you can make it yourself with our easy recipe.

SAUCES & DRESSINGS

HOMEMADE TOMATO KETCHUP

**MAKES ABOUT 750ML (1¼ PINTS/3 CUPS)
PREP 15 MINUTES
COOK 45–50 MINUTES**

2.5kg (5lb 9oz) ripe tomatoes, skinned and deseeded
4 garlic cloves, crushed
1 tbsp grated fresh root ginger
1 tbsp yellow mustard seeds
1 tsp celery seeds
½ tsp ground mace
½ tsp sea salt
¼ tsp ground black peppercorns
a pinch of ground cloves
2 tbsp soft brown sugar
2 tbsp tomato paste
150ml (5fl oz/scant ¾ cup) red wine vinegar
a dash of hot sauce, e.g. Tabasco or sriracha

VARIATIONS
- Use apple cider vinegar.
- Add some diced red chillies for a hot flavour.
- Add some ground allspice, paprika or cinnamon.

HOW ABOUT GOING THE WHOLE HOG AND MAKING YOUR OWN KETCHUP? IT'S SO DELICIOUS AND WILL ENHANCE THE FLAVOUR OF SO MANY OF YOUR FAVOURITE DISHES. IT'S EASY TO PREPARE AND MAKE BUT YOU MUST CHECK ON IT REGULARLY WHILE IT'S COOKING TO MAKE SURE IT DOES NOT BURN – IT'S WELL WORTH THE EFFORT.

1. Put all the ingredients into a preserving pan or a large heavy-based saucepan and stir well. Set over a high heat and bring to the boil, stirring to dissolve the sugar.
2. Reduce the heat to medium-high and cook, checking the pan and stirring frequently so that the sauce does not catch and burn, until it reduces to a thick sauce. This may take up to 45 minutes or even longer.
3. Transfer to a blender and blitz to a purée. If you want a really smooth ketchup, you can pass the purée through a fine sieve. Check the seasoning and add more salt and pepper, hot sauce or sugar, if wished
4. Transfer to a jug and use a funnel to pour the ketchup into sterilized jars or bottles. Seal and store in a cool place for up to 3 months.

TIP:
To sterilize bottles or jars, wash them well in hot, soapy water, then rinse and place them together with the lids on a baking tray in a preheated oven at 170°C (150°C fan)/325°F/gas 3 for 15 minutes.

6 ripe tomatoes, diced
½ red onion, diced
1 garlic clove, crushed
2 hot chillies, e.g. jalapeños
  (fresh or bottled), diced
a handful of coriander
  (cilantro), chopped
2 tbsp ketchup
juice of 1 lime
1 small, ripe avocado,
  peeled, stoned (pitted)
  and diced
a pinch of fine sea salt

VARIATIONS

- **Use spring onions (scallions) instead of red onion.**
- **Use garlic powder to taste instead of a fresh clove.**
- **Use chopped cherry or baby plum tomatoes.**
- **Add some diced mango or papaya.**
- **Add some hot sauce, e.g. sriracha.**

VEGAN

KETCHUP PICO DE GALLO

THIS MAKES A DELICIOUS DIP FOR TORTILLA CHIPS OR RAW VEGETABLE STICKS, OR YOU CAN SMEAR IT OVER SANDWICHES AND WRAPS, USE AS A TOPPING FOR NACHOS, FAJITAS, BURRITOS AND TACOS, OR SERVE WITH KEBABS, STEAKS, CHICKEN, CHOPS, SAUSAGES, GRILLED HALLOUMI AND TOFU – IT'S SO VERSATILE. ADDING KETCHUP GIVES IT A REAL KICK AND EXTRA PIQUANCY.

1. Mix the tomatoes, red onion, garlic, chillies and coriander in a bowl. Stir in the ketchup and lime juice and leave for 15 minutes for the flavours to mingle.
2. Stir in the avocado and season to taste with salt. Transfer to a serving bowl.

TIP:

If you're making this ahead, don't add the avocado until you're ready to serve. It will keep well in a sealed container in the fridge for 2–3 days without the avocado.

MAKES 400ML (14FL OZ/ GENEROUS 1½ CUPS)
PREP 5 MINUTES
COOK 5 MINUTES

300ml (½ pint/1¼ cups) ketchup
3 tbsp soft brown sugar
3 tbsp red wine or apple cider vinegar
2 tbsp Worcestershire sauce
1 tbsp soy sauce
1 tbsp Dijon or wholegrain mustard
juice of ½ lemon
1–2 tsp smoked paprika
½ tsp garlic powder
salt and freshly ground black pepper

VEGAN

BARBECUE SAUCE

THIS SAUCE IS SO EASY TO MAKE. YOU CAN RUSTLE IT UP IN 10 MINUTES FROM A FEW BASIC STORE-CUPBOARD INGREDIENTS. SERVE IT WITH GRILLED STEAK, CHICKEN, PORK OR LAMB CHOPS, RIBS, SAUSAGES, PRAWNS (SHRIMP) AND GRILLED VEGETABLES. OR YOU CAN BRUSH IT OVER THEM WHILE THEY ARE COOKING FOR A DELICIOUS GLAZE.

1. Put all the ingredients into a small saucepan and stir well.
2. Set over a medium heat and when the sauce starts to bubble gently, give it a stir and cook for 5 minutes. Check the seasoning and serve warm.

TIP:
You can use the cold sauce as a marinade for chicken and spare ribs.

MAKES 180ML (6FL OZ/
¾ CUP)
PREP 5 MINUTES
CHILL 1 HOUR

120g (4oz/½ cup)
   mayonnaise
2 tbsp ketchup
2 tbsp sweet pickle or dill
   pickle relish
1 tbsp white wine or apple
   cider vinegar
1 tbsp finely diced onion or
   spring onions (scallions)
1 tsp sugar
salt and freshly ground
   black pepper

VEGAN

THOUSAND ISLAND DRESSING

YOU CAN USE THIS CREAMY, PIQUANT SAUCE FOR
DRESSING ICEBERG LETTUCE AND CRISP SALADS OR
EVEN AS A COCKTAIL SAUCE FOR SEAFOOD. FOR A
RUSSIAN DRESSING, OMIT THE SWEET PICKLE AND
DICED ONION AND USE HORSERADISH SAUCE AND A
DASH OF CHILLI SAUCE INSTEAD.

1. Put all the ingredients into a bowl and stir well to combine.
   Season to taste with salt and pepper.
2. Cover and chill in the fridge for at least 1 hour before
   serving. This will keep well in an airtight container in the
   fridge for up to 5 days.

MAKES 150ML (5FL OZ/
SCANT ¾ CUP)
PREP 5 MINUTES

120ml (4fl oz/½ cup) ketchup
2 tbsp hot sauce
1–2 tbsp horseradish sauce
juice of ½ small lemon
a few drops of
   Worcestershire sauce
salt and freshly ground black
   pepper

VEGAN

SEAFOOD COCKTAIL SAUCE

THIS TANGY SAUCE IS PERFECT WITH BOILED OR
GRILLED (BROILED) PRAWNS (SHRIMP), CRAB,
LOBSTER, FRIED FISH OR EVEN BURGERS, OR EVEN AS
A DIP FOR RAW VEGETABLES OR TORTILLA CHIPS. EASY
TO MAKE, IT HAS ONLY FIVE INGREDIENTS.

1. Put the ketchup, hot sauce and 1 tablespoon horseradish
   in a bowl with the lemon juice and Worcestershire sauce.
   Mix until well blended. Season to taste, adding more
   horseradish if it's not hot enough for you.
2. Transfer to a small bowl and serve with a platter of seafood.
   Store in the fridge in an airtight container for up to 2 weeks.

VARIATIONS
- Stir in mayo or cream
  cheese.
- Use fiery Tabasco.

KETCHUP MARINADE

**MAKES 180ML
(6FL OZ/¾ CUP)
PREP 10 MINUTES
CHILL 2–4 HOURS**

4 tbsp ketchup
4 tbsp clear honey
2 tbsp soy sauce
3 tbsp soft brown sugar
2 garlic cloves, crushed
1 tsp dried onion flakes
salt and freshly ground
black pepper

TIP:

For maximum flavour and
tenderness, marinate the
meat or chicken overnight.

THIS SIMPLE MARINADE IS PERFECT FOR KEEPING CHICKEN BREASTS, WINGS AND DRUMSTICKS, STEAK AND PORK CHOPS TENDER AND JUICY AS WELL AS ADDING A SWEET, TANGY FLAVOUR. IF YOU WANT TO MAKE IT IN ADVANCE, IT WILL KEEP WELL IN THE FRIDGE IN A SEALED CONTAINER FOR UP TO 5 DAYS.

1. Mix everything together in a large glass bowl until well blended.
2. Add the chicken or meat to be marinated and stir well until it is thoroughly coated with the marinade.
3. Cover and chill in the fridge for at least 2 hours – preferably 4 hours for maximum flavour – before baking or grilling (broiling). Baste with any leftover marinade while it cooks.

VEGAN

KETCHUP VINAIGRETTE

**MAKES 180ML
(6FL OZ/¾ CUP)
PREP 5 MINUTES**

4 tbsp light olive oil
3 tbsp red wine vinegar
3 tbsp clear honey
2 tbsp ketchup
a dash of Worcestershire
sauce
2 spring onions (scallions),
finely chopped
a few chives or sprigs of
parsley, finely chopped

NEVER THOUGHT ABOUT ADDING KETCHUP TO A VINAIGRETTE? NOW'S THE TIME TO TRY. PERFECT FOR CRISP LETTUCE, TOMATO AND AVOCADO SALADS.

Put all the ingredients in a screwtop jar. Screw on the lid and shake until completely blended. This will keep well in the fridge for 3–4 days.

VARIATIONS
• Add a dash of Tabasco or another hot sauce.
• Use a diced shallot or red onion instead of spring onions.
• Add 2 tsp honey mustard.

STEAK SAUCE

**MAKES 200ML (7FL OZ/
GENEROUS ¾ CUP)
PREP 5 MINUTES
COOK 20 MINUTES**

120ml (4fl oz/½ cup)
  ketchup
2 tbsp apple cider vinegar
juice of ½ lemon
2 tbsp soy sauce
1 tbsp soft brown sugar
2 tsp Dijon mustard
¼ tsp garlic powder
a dash of hot sauce, e.g.
  Tabasco
salt and freshly ground
  black pepper

VARIATIONS

- Add a few drops
  of Worcestershire
  sauce.
- Use red or white
  wine vinegar.
- Add a good pinch
  of Chinese five-
  spice powder.
- Use crushed fresh
  garlic instead of
  garlic powder.
- For a fiery flavour,
  add some diced
  fresh chilli or more
  hot sauce.

INSTEAD OF BUYING A BOTTLE OF STEAK SAUCE FROM THE SUPERMARKET, YOU CAN MAKE YOUR OWN AT HOME WITHOUT ALL THE ADDITIVES AND PRESERVATIVES. THIS KEEPS WELL IN THE FRIDGE FOR UP TO TWO WEEKS SO YOU COULD MAKE DOUBLE THE SUGGESTED QUANTITY. SERVE IT WITH BURGERS, CHOPS AND SAUSAGES AS WELL AS STEAK.

1. Put all the ingredients into a saucepan and stir well.
2. Set the pan over a high heat and bring to the boil. Reduce the heat to low and simmer gently, stirring from time to time, for 20 minutes, or until the sauce reduces and thickens.
3. Set aside to cool. When the sauce is cold, transfer it to a bottle or an airtight container. Store in the fridge.

CANAPÉS

ROASTED RED PEPPER AND KETCHUP HUMMUS

SERVES 4
PREP 10 MINUTES

1 × 400g (14oz) tin
chickpeas, drained and
rinsed
3 garlic cloves, crushed
2 tbsp tahini
2 tbsp olive oil
grated zest and juice of ½
lemon
½ tsp ground cumin
2 bottled roasted red (bell)
peppers, drained and
rinsed
2 tbsp ketchup
2 tbsp 0% fat Greek yoghurt
salt and freshly ground
black pepper
paprika for dusting

VARIATIONS
- Use cumin seeds
  instead of ground
  cumin.
- Sprinkle with red
  pepper or crushed
  dried chilli flakes.
- Drizzle with olive oil
  and lemon juice.

THE PEPPERS AND KETCHUP ADD COLOUR, A DISTINCTIVE TANGY FLAVOUR AND A HINT OF SWEETNESS TO HOMEMADE HUMMUS. SERVE IT AS A SPREAD OR AS A DIP WITH SOME RAW VEGETABLES, TORTILLA OR POTATO CHIPS, WARM FLATBREADS OR PITTA BREAD.

1. Blitz the chickpeas, garlic, tahini, olive oil, lemon zest and juice, cumin, red peppers and ketchup to a thick paste in a food processor or blender. If it's too thick, add a little more olive oil or lemon juice to get the desired consistency.
2. Spoon into a bowl and stir in the yoghurt. Season with salt and pepper, then lightly dust with paprika.

TIP:
For extra flavour, use 2 fresh red peppers. Char over a gas flame or pop under a hot grill (broiler), turning occasionally, until tender and charred. Peel off the skin and discard the stalks and seeds before blitzing with the other ingredients.

SERVES 4
PREP 10 MINUTES

½ red onion, diced
1 hot red chilli, diced
1 garlic clove, crushed
½ tsp sea salt
2 ripe avocados
juice of 1 lime
a handful of coriander
 (cilantro), chopped
1 ripe tomato, deseeded and
 diced
1–2 tbsp ketchup
freshly ground black pepper

VARIATIONS
- **Use spring onions (scallions) instead of red onion.**
- **If you like it hot, add more chillies.**
- **For a creamy texture, stir in 1–2 tbsp soured cream or Greek yoghurt.**

VEGAN

CHUNKY KETCHUP GUACAMOLE

ADDING KETCHUP TO GUACAMOLE GIVES IT A REAL KICK AND AN EXTRA DIMENSION. AND SWIRLING IT THROUGH THE MASHED AVOCADO MIXTURE AT THE END JUST BEFORE SERVING ADDS COLOUR WITHOUT SPOILING THE LOVELY FRESH GREEN OF THE DIP. YOU CAN USE ANY FRESH CHILLIES – JALAPEÑOS, SCOTCH BONNET OR THE LITTLE THAI BIRD'S-EYE ONES.

1. Crush the red onion, chilli, garlic and salt together with a pestle and mortar.
2. Cut the avocados in half and remove the stones (pits). Scoop out the flesh and mash roughly with a fork. Don't overdo it – it should be slightly chunky rather than too smooth. Gently stir in the lime juice.
3. Add the coriander, crushed red onion mixture and the diced tomato and mix everything together. Add a grinding of black pepper and swirl in the ketchup.
4. Transfer the guacamole to a serving bowl and use as a dip for tortilla chips or as a topping for Mexican dishes.

CHEESY NACHOS WITH KETCHUP

SERVES 4
PREP 10 MINUTES
COOK 10 MINUTES

200g (7oz) salted corn
  tortilla chips
4 ripe tomatoes, deseeded
  and chopped
1 × 400g (14oz) tin black
  beans, drained and rinsed
1 × 200g (7oz) tin sweetcorn
  kernels, drained
a bunch of spring onions
  (scallions), thinly sliced
2 fresh red or green chillies,
  thinly sliced
2 tbsp ketchup
150g (5oz/1 cup) hot salsa
100g (4oz/1 cup) grated
  Cheddar cheese
1 quantity Chunky Ketchup
  Guacamole (see page 23)

SERVE THESE TEX–MEX NACHOS AT PARTIES, WITH DRINKS BEFORE DINNER OR AS PART OF A HOT BUFFET. WE'VE ADDED KETCHUP TO THE SALSA TO SPICE IT UP EVEN MORE BUT YOU COULD TRY DRIZZLING IT OVER THE VEGETABLES BEFORE TOPPING WITH THE SALSA AND CHEESE.

1. Preheat the oven to 200°C (180°C fan)/400°F/gas 6.
2. Put half of the tortilla chips in a shallow ovenproof dish and sprinkle with half of the tomatoes, black beans, sweetcorn, spring onions and chillies. Cover with the remaining tortilla chips and top with the remaining vegetables and beans.
3. Stir the ketchup into the salsa and spoon half of it over the top. Sprinkle with the grated cheese.
4. Bake in the preheated oven for about 10 minutes until the cheese melts and is bubbling.
5. Spoon the remaining salsa and the guacamole over the top and serve immediately.

VARIATIONS

- Use thinly sliced pickled jalapeños instead of fresh chillies.
- Instead of the beans and veg, use chili made with minced (ground) beef and layer in the same way.
- Substitute Monterey Jack or mozzarella for the Cheddar.

SERVES 4
PREP 10 MINUTES
COOK 10 MINUTES

6 tbsp olive oil
1 tbsp smoked paprika
a good pinch of crushed
   dried chilli flakes
1 tbsp ketchup
a few drops of piri piri sauce
4 garlic cloves, crushed
a handful of flat-leaf
   parsley, finely chopped
16 peeled raw king prawns
   (jumbo shrimp)
crusty bread, to serve

VARIATIONS
- Add some finely
  chopped onion
  or spring onions
  (scallions).
- Use small prawns
  instead of large ones.
- Use a diced fresh
  red chilli instead of
  dried flakes.

SPANISH PIRI PIRI KETCHUP TAPAS

RAMEKINS OF SIZZLING SPICY AND SMOKY PRAWNS (SHRIMP) ARE SERVED IN EVERY TAPAS BAR IN SOUTHERN SPAIN, BUT ADDING A SPOONFUL OF KETCHUP MAKES THEM EVEN MORE PIQUANT AND DELECTABLE. TO BE REALLY AUTHENTIC, SERVE WITH A GLASS OF CHILLED WHITE WINE OR MANZANILLA SHERRY.

1. Preheat the oven to 220°C (200°C fan)/425°F/gas 7.
2. Pour the oil into 4 individual shallow ovenproof dishes (ceramic or terracotta ones are best). Place on a baking tray (cookie sheet) in the preheated oven for 5 minutes, or until the oil is really hot.
3. Mix together the paprika, chilli flakes, ketchup, piri piri sauce, garlic and most of the parsley. Stir into the hot oil and then add 4 prawns to each dish, turning them over in the oil.
4. Cook in the oven for 5 minutes, or until the prawns are pink on both sides and the spicy oil is sizzling.
5. Serve immediately while the prawns are piping hot, sprinkled with the remaining parsley and with some crusty bread to mop up the delicious oil.

5 tbsp olive oil
500g (1lb 2oz) aubergines (eggplants), cubed
1 red onion, chopped
3 garlic cloves, crushed
2 celery sticks, diced
1 red (bell) pepper, deseeded and cut into chunks
450g (1lb) ripe tomatoes, skinned and chopped
85ml (3fl oz/⅓ cup) red wine vinegar
3 tbsp ketchup
30g (1oz/scant ¼ cup) capers
60g (2oz/½ cup) stoned (pitted) olives
60g (2oz/½ cup) sultanas (seedless golden raisins)
1 tbsp sugar
45g (1½oz/scant ½ cup) pine nuts
a handful of flat-leaf parsley, chopped
sea salt and freshly ground black pepper

VARIATIONS

- Add some harissa or diced fresh chilli.
- Stir in some ground cumin or cinnamon.
- Add the juice of 1 lemon before serving.

VEGAN

KETCHUP CAPONATA

THIS CLASSIC SICILIAN DISH IS NOTED FOR ITS AGRODOLCE (SWEET AND SOUR) FLAVOURS. IT CAN BE SERVED AS A DIP OR AS A TOPPING FOR BRUSCHETTA, CROSTINI OR CRACKERS. THE ADDITION OF KETCHUP ENHANCES THE SHARPNESS OF THE VINEGAR AND HELPS TO BRING OUT THE SWEETNESS OF THE SULTANAS AND TOMATOES. YOU WILL NEED A PAN WITH A LID.

1. Heat the oil in a large deep frying pan (skillet) set over a medium heat. Cook the aubergines, stirring occasionally, for 5 minutes, or until tender and golden brown. Remove and drain on kitchen paper (paper towels).
2. Add the onion, garlic, celery and red pepper and cook, stirring occasionally, for 6–8 minutes, or until tender. Stir in the tomatoes, vinegar and ketchup and lower the heat to a simmer. Add the capers, olives and sultanas. Stir in the sugar, return the aubergines to the pan and season to taste.
3. Cover and simmer over the lowest possible heat for 30 minutes, checking occasionally, until the vegetables are really tender and the liquid has reduced and thickened. Moisten with a little water if necessary.
4. Meanwhile, toast the pine nuts in a dry frying pan over a medium to high heat for 1–2 minutes, tossing them gently, until aromatic and golden brown. Remove from the pan before they catch and burn.
5. Stir most of the parsley into the caponata and transfer to a serving bowl. Sprinkle the rest over the top along with the pine nuts. Serve lukewarm or cold.

VEGAN JACKFRUIT CARNITAS

**MAKES 8 TORTILLAS
PREP 15 MINUTES
COOK 20 MINUTES**

2 × 400g (14oz) tins green jackfruit in brine, drained
2 tbsp olive oil
1 red onion, finely chopped
4 garlic cloves, crushed
1 green jalapeño pepper (fresh, tinned or bottled), diced
2 tbsp ketchup
1 tbsp dark soy sauce
2 tsp demerara sugar
1 tsp ground cumin
½ tsp sweet smoked paprika
¼ tsp salt
8 small soft tortillas wraps
Ketchup Pico de Gallo (see page 14) and/or Chunky Ketchup Guacamole (see page 23), to serve

VARIATIONS

- Add crisp lettuce, tomato, tinned beans or sweetcorn.
- Add chilli powder, or smoked paprika.
- Add grated cheese (dairy or vegan).
- Serve with soured cream, yoghurt or vegan cashew cream.

'FAUX MEAT' IS ALL THE RAGE AND THE GREAT THING ABOUT JACKFRUIT IS THAT, ALTHOUGH IT IS TECHNICALLY A FRUIT, ITS TEXTURE IS SIMILAR TO THAT OF PORK OR CHICKEN WHEN IT'S COOKED. AND BECAUSE IT HAS A BLAND, NEUTRAL TASTE, KETCHUP, TOGETHER WITH SOY, TAMARI AND BARBECUE SAUCES, ENLIVENS ITS FLAVOUR AND MAKES IT A DELICIOUS AND ECONOMICAL ALTERNATIVE TO MEAT.

1. Pat the jackfruit with kitchen paper (paper towels) to dry them and then cut down through the core into thin slices. Gently squeeze dry with kitchen paper. They must be as dry as possible so they'll crisp up when you cook them.
2. Heat 1 tablespoon oil in a large frying pan (skillet) set over a medium heat. Add the onion, garlic and jalapeño and cook, stirring occasionally, for 6–8 minutes until tender and golden.
3. Reduce the heat to low and stir in the jackfruit, ketchup and soy sauce. Cook for at least 5 minutes, stirring frequently, until the mixture seems quite dry and no longer moist.
4. Shred the jackfruit with a fork and add the remaining oil together with the sugar, spices and salt. Cook for 5 minutes, or until the jackfruit caramelizes and is crispy and golden brown.
5. Meanwhile, heat the tortillas in a clean frying pan for 1–2 minutes each side, or by warming them in a low oven.
6. Divide the crispy jackfruit mixture between the tortillas and top with some pico de gallo and/or guacamole. Roll them up and serve immediately.

MAKES 8
PREP 10 MINUTES
COOK 15 MINUTES

4 English muffins
125g (4½oz/1¼ cups) grated
   mozzarella cheese
8 wafer-thin slices of
   prosciutto (Parma ham)
wild rocket (arugula), to
   garnish

PIZZA SAUCE
1 tbsp olive oil
1 small red onion, finely
   diced
2 garlic cloves, crushed
3 tbsp ketchup
1 tbsp tomato paste
freshly ground black pepper

VARIATIONS
- Add a pinch of dried
  basil or oregano to
  the pizza sauce.
- Add some pitted
  black olives, sautéed
  mushrooms or bottled
  charred red or yellow
  (bell) peppers.
- Add some sliced
  pepperoni or salami.
- Vegetarians can omit
  the prosciutto.

VEGETARIAN

SPEEDY KETCHUP MINI PIZZAS

THE BASES YOU USE FOR THESE YUMMY PIZZAS DEPEND ON WHETHER YOU ARE SERVING THEM AS A CANAPÉ, A SNACK OR A LIGHT MEAL. WE HAVE USED TOASTED ENGLISH MUFFINS FOR THE BASES BUT YOU COULD SUBSTITUTE CRUMPETS, MINI PITTAS OR SMALL TORTILLAS CRISPED UP IN A FRYING PAN (SKILLET) OR RIDGED GRIDDLE PAN, OR BOUGHT MINI PIZZA BASES OR EVEN BLINIS.

1. Preheat the grill (broiler) to high.
2. Make the pizza sauce: heat the olive oil in a pan over a low to medium heat and cook the onion and garlic for 8–10 minutes until softened. Stir in the ketchup and tomato paste and season to taste with black pepper.
3. Split the muffins in half and toast them lightly. Spread the pizza sauce thinly over them and sprinkle with mozzarella.
4. Pop under the preheated grill for 5 minutes, or until the cheese melts and bubbles.
5. Top each muffin with a folded slice of prosciutto and a few sprigs of rocket. Serve immediately.

MAKES 12
PREP 20 MINUTES
COOK 5 MINUTES

50g (2oz) vermicelli noodles
(dried weight)
1 tbsp vegetable or sesame oil
2 red (bell) peppers, cut into
thin matchsticks
1 large carrot, cut into thin
matchsticks
2cm (¾in) piece of fresh root
ginger, peeled and diced
100g (3½oz) spring greens,
kale or spinach, shredded
100g (3½oz/1 cup)
beansprouts
300g (10oz) cooked peeled
small prawns (shrimp)
4 tbsp soy sauce
1 tbsp ketchup
a handful of coriander
(cilantro), chopped
12 small soft lettuce leaves
small bundle of chives
(optional)
12 round rice paper wrappers

THAI DIPPING SAUCE

2 tbsp soy sauce
2 tbsp nam pla (Thai fish
sauce)
2 tbsp ketchup
1 tbsp rice wine vinegar
1 tbsp lemon juice or water
1 tsp hot chilli or sesame oil
1 tsp sugar
1 garlic clove, crushed

FRESH SPRING ROLLS WITH THAI DIPPING SAUCE

YOU CAN MAKE DELICIOUS FRESH SPRING ROLLS WITH RICE PAPER WRAPPERS – THEY ARE MUCH HEALTHIER THAN FRIED ONES AND PERFECT FOR PARTIES OR WITH PRE-DINNER DRINKS.

1. Put the noodles in a shallow bowl and cover with warm water. Leave for 2–3 minutes and then drain. (Or follow the instructions on the packet.)
2. Make the Thai dipping sauce: mix all the ingredients together until well blended. Cover and chill in the fridge while you make the spring rolls.
3. Heat the oil in a wok or large frying pan (skillet) over a high heat. Stir-fry the peppers, carrot and ginger for 2 minutes, then add the greens, beansprouts and prawns and stir-fry for 2 minutes. Stir in the soy sauce, ketchup and coriander.
4. Divide the noodles between the lettuce leaves and roll up.
5. Fill a bowl with tepid water and position it near you while you assemble the spring rolls.
6. Dip a rice paper wrapper into the water until pliable. Lay it out flat on a clean work surface. Add a rolled up lettuce leaf and some prawn filling, leaving a broad edge around it.
7. Fold the sides of the wrapper over the filling to enclose it and then roll up like a parcel. Place on a serving plate seam-side down, or secure by tying a long chive stem around it. Make the remaining spring rolls in the same way and serve with the dipping sauce.

VARIATIONS
- Add some sliced chilli and spring onions (scallions).
- Vegetarians can omit the prawns and add extra vegetables or noodles.

31

EASY KETCHUP SUSHI

300g (10oz/1¼ cups) sushi rice (dried weight)

2 tbsp rice vinegar

1 tsp sugar

150g (5oz) peeled cooked prawns (shrimp), roughly chopped

2 tbsp light mayonnaise

1 tbsp ketchup

1 tbsp wasabi, plus extra to serve

4 sheets of nori seaweed

1 small ripe avocado

a bunch of chives

1–2 tbsp toasted sesame seeds

light soy sauce, to serve

VARIATIONS

- Dice the avocado or mash it with the wasabi and a squeeze of lemon juice.
- Add some cucumber, sliced into very thin strips.
- Serve with a dip of mayo, ketchup and hot sauce or wasabi.

SUSHI IS SURPRISINGLY QUICK AND EASY TO MAKE AND IS GREAT FOR CANAPÉS. IT CAN SOMETIMES BE QUITE BLAND BUT MIXING THE PRAWN (SHRIMP) FILLING WITH MAYO, KETCHUP AND WASABI GIVES IT A REAL KICK. FOR MORE HEAT, ADD EXTRA WASABI, TASTING AS YOU GO ALONG.

1. Cook the rice according to the directions on the packet until it's tender and all the water has been absorbed – this should take 10–15 minutes. Stir in the vinegar and sugar, cover the pan and leave to cool until the rice is at room temperature.
2. Mix the prawns with the mayonnaise, ketchup and wasabi in a bowl.
3. Place the nori sheets, shiny-side down, on a bamboo sushi mat or work surface covered with cling film (plastic wrap). Spread the cooled rice over the sheets, leaving a 1cm (½in) border along the long edges.
4. Halve, stone (pit) and peel the avocado and slice it very thinly. Spoon one-quarter of the prawn mixture on top of the rice. Lay a few chives on top and then cover with the avocado.
5. Using the cling film and sushi mat (if applicable), lift the long bottom edge over the filling and roll up firmly towards the top, pressing down and sprinkling with sesame seeds as you go. When you reach the top, moisten the edge of the nori with water to seal. Repeat with the remaining sheets to make 4 rolls. If wished, wrap the rolls in cling film and keep in the fridge until ready to serve.
6. Cut each roll into 8 rounds and serve with wasabi and light soy sauce for sprinkling or dipping.

CEVICHE

500g (1lb 2oz) skinned and boned white fish fillets, e.g. sea bass, bream or halibut
240ml (8fl oz/1 cup) freshly squeezed lemon or lime juice
1 small red onion, diced
1 garlic clove, crushed
400g (14oz) ripe red tomatoes, deseeded and diced
2 tbsp ketchup
1–2 tbsp hot sauce
1 tbsp olive oil
a bunch of coriander (cilantro), chopped
1 jalapeño chilli, diced
salt and freshly ground black pepper
crispy grilled (broiled) tortillas, to serve

IN THIS MEXICAN DISH, RAW FISH IS CURED IN FRESH CITRUS JUICE AND THEN ADDED TO A FRESH TOMATO DRESSING SPICED WITH CHILLI AND HOT SAUCE. IT'S IMPORTANT TO USE REALLY FRESH GOOD–QUALITY FISH FOR THE BEST FLAVOUR.

1. Cut the fish into 1–2cm (½–¾in) cubes and place in a large glass dish. Pour the lemon or lime juice over it and stir gently to coat all over. Cover and set aside to marinate in a cool place for at least 1 hour (but no longer than 2 hours), by which time the fish should be 'cooked' and opaque.
2. Mix the onion, garlic, tomatoes, ketchup, hot sauce, oil, coriander and chilli in a glass bowl. Season with salt and pepper.
3. Remove the fish from the marinade and stir into the tomato mixture. Serve with crispy tortillas.

VARIATIONS
- Use peeled, raw prawns (shrimp) or tuna instead of white fish.
- Add some diced cucumber or avocado to the tomato mixture.
- For more heat, add Scotch bonnet chillies.
- Add some aji amarillo paste for an authentic Mexican flavour.
- Use orange juice as well as lime or lemon.
- Serve on bite-sized crackers, toasts or blinis.

BREAKFASTS & BRUNCHES

SERVES 4
PREP 10 MINUTES
COOK 40–45 MINUTES

4 large corn tortilla wraps
2 tbsp olive oil
4 medium free-range eggs
a good pinch of crushed
    dried chilli flakes
a bunch of spring onions
    (scallions), thinly sliced
1 large ripe avocado,
    peeled, stoned (pitted)
    and diced
juice of 1 lime
100g (4oz/1 cup) grated
    Cheddar or Monterey
    Jack cheese
soured cream, to serve

SPICY TOMATO SAUCE

2 tbsp olive oil
1 red onion, chopped
1 red (bell) pepper,
    deseeded and diced
3 garlic cloves, crushed
1 red chilli, diced
a pinch of cumin seeds
2 × 400g (14oz) tins
    chopped tomatoes
60ml (2fl oz/¼ cup) ketchup
a pinch of sugar
a dash of hot sauce, e.g.
    Tabasco or habanero
salt and freshly ground
    black pepper

VEGETARIAN

BAJA BRUNCH

THIS MEXICAN DISH IS OFTEN SERVED IN BAJA AND SOUTHERN CALIFORNIA. YOU CAN ENJOY IT ANY TIME OF DAY – FOR A LIGHT LUNCH OR SUPPER AS WELL AS FOR BREAKFAST OR BRUNCH.

1. Make the spicy tomato sauce: heat the oil in a large frying pan (skillet) set over a low heat. Add the onion, pepper, garlic and chilli and cook for 8–10 minutes, or until tender.
2. Stir in the cumin seeds and cook for 1 minute. Add the tomatoes, ketchup and sugar and simmer, stirring occasionally, for 15 minutes, or until reduced and thickened. Add hot sauce to taste and season with salt and pepper.
3. Heat the tortillas in a large frying pan set over a low to medium heat for 1–2 minutes each side, or until golden and slightly crisp. Remove and keep warm.
4. Turn up the heat and add the oil to the pan. Fry the eggs until the whites are set and crisp around the edges but the yolks are still runny. To set the film on top of the yolks, spoon some hot oil over them or flash under a hot grill (broiler).
5. Place a tortilla on each serving plate. Spoon some spicy tomato sauce over the top and then add a fried egg. Scatter with the chilli flakes and spring onions. Toss the avocado in the lime juice and sprinkle over the top with the grated cheese. Serve immediately with soured cream on the side.

TIP:
Make the sauce ahead and reheat for breakfast or brunch.

VARIATIONS
• Scatter some chopped coriander (cilantro) over the eggs.
• Add some diced chorizo or bacon to the tomato sauce.
• Serve with soured cream and guacamole.

BREAKFAST KETCHUP BURRITOS

SERVES 4
PREP 15 MINUTES
COOK 10 MINUTES

8 thin slices of streaky bacon
4 large tortilla wraps
6 medium free-range eggs
4 tbsp milk
85g (3oz/scant ½ cup)
   grated Cheddar cheese
a few sprigs of coriander
   (cilantro), chopped
2 tbsp olive oil
4 spring onions (scallions),
   thinly sliced
1 red chilli, deseeded and
   diced
8 tbsp Ketchup Pico de Gallo
   (see page 14)
salt and freshly ground
   black pepper
hot sauce or ketchup, for
   drizzling

VARIATIONS
- Use crushed dried chilli flakes instead of fresh chilli.
- Add sautéed diced cherry tomatoes or mushrooms.
- Instead of adding the cheese to the eggs, sprinkle it over before rolling the tortillas.

THESE TASTY BURRITOS WILL MAKE YOUR WEEKEND BREAKFAST OR BRUNCH MORE SPECIAL. IF YOU LIKE THEM REALLY CRISPY, YOU CAN TOAST THEM QUICKLY IN A HOT PAN FOR A FEW SECONDS AFTER FOLDING AND ROLLING THEM.

1. Cook the bacon in a frying pan (skillet) or under a hot grill (broiler) until it's golden brown and crisp. Remove and drain on kitchen paper (paper towels).
2. Add the tortillas to the hot pan and heat in the bacon fat over a low to medium heat for a few seconds. Remove and keep warm.
3. In a bowl, whisk the eggs and milk together, then beat in the cheese and coriander. Season lightly with salt and pepper.
4. Heat the oil in a non-stick frying pan set over a low to medium heat. Cook the spring onions and chilli for 3 minutes, or until softened.
5. Reduce the heat to very low and add the beaten egg mixture. Stir with a wooden spoon, drawing the mixture in from the sides of the pan to the middle. As soon as the eggs start to scramble and set, remove the pan from the heat.
6. Place a tortilla wrap on each plate and spread with the ketchup pico de gallo. Crumble the crispy bacon over the top and add the scrambled eggs. Fold the sides of each tortilla over the filling and roll it up from the other side. Serve immediately, drizzled with hot sauce or ketchup.

TIP:
If you don't have any Ketchup Pico de Gallo, just spread each tortilla with 1–2 tablespoons ketchup and 1 tablespoon hot salsa.

SERVES 4
PREP 5 MINUTES
COOK 10 MINUTES

2 tbsp olive oil
4 large flat mushrooms
2 large beefsteak tomatoes
4 medium free-range eggs
2 English muffins
4 tbsp tomato ketchup
sea salt and freshly ground
   black pepper
snipped chives, for
   sprinkling (optional)

VARIATIONS
- **Use toasted crumpets instead of muffins.**
- **Add some crispy bacon or sliced sausages.**
- **Fill the mushrooms with creamed spinach instead of eggs.**

VEGETARIAN
ENGLISH MUFFIN BREAKFAST STACKS

THESE STACKS ARE A HEALTHY AND NUTRITIOUS WAY TO START THE DAY. AND THEY ARE SO QUICK AND EASY TO MAKE – LESS THAN 15 MINUTES – THAT YOU'LL BE ABLE TO TREAT YOURSELF TO A COOKED BREAKFAST EVEN ON A WORK DAY.

1. Heat the oil in a large non-stick frying pan (skillet) set over a medium heat. Cook the mushrooms for 5 minutes, turning them halfway through, or until tender and golden brown. Remove from the pan, drain on kitchen paper (paper towels) and keep warm.
2. Cut the tomatoes in half horizontally and add to the same pan. Cook for 2–3 minutes, then turn them over and cook until tender and starting to brown.
3. Meanwhile, bring a saucepan of water to the boil, then reduce the heat to a bare simmer and gently break the eggs into the hot water. Cover the pan and leave to cook over the lowest possible heat for 3–4 minutes, or until the whites are set but the yolks are still runny. Remove carefully with a slotted spoon and drain on kitchen paper.
4. While the eggs are poaching, split the muffins in half and lightly toast them.
5. To assemble the stacks, spread the ketchup over each muffin and place a tomato half on top. Cover with a mushroom (hollow side up) and fill with a poached egg. Season with salt and pepper and sprinkle with chives. Serve immediately.

TIP:
Instead of frying the mushrooms and tomatoes, brush lightly with oil and cook under a hot grill (broiler).

2 tbsp olive oil
1 red onion, diced
2 red (bell) peppers,
   deseeded and diced
3 garlic cloves, crushed
1 red chilli, diced
1 tsp smoked paprika
1 tsp ground cumin
2 × 400g (14oz) tins chopped
   tomatoes
2 tbsp tomato paste
120ml (4fl oz/½ cup) ketchup
a pinch of sugar
a handful of coriander
   (cilantro), chopped
4 large free-range eggs
50g (2oz/⅓ cup) feta cheese
salt and freshly ground black
   pepper
warm pitta breads,
   flatbreads or challah
   bread, to serve

VARIATIONS
- Add diced aubergine
  (eggplant) or olives.
- Add chopped spinach
  or baby spinach
  leaves.
- Serve drizzled with
  tahini sauce.

VEGETARIAN

KETCHUP SHAKSHUKA

THIS TRADITIONAL DISH OF POACHED EGGS IN A SPICY TOMATO SAUCE IS SERVED FOR BREAKFAST THROUGHOUT THE MIDDLE EAST AND NORTH AFRICA. THE KETCHUP MAY SEEM LIKE HERESY TO THE PURISTS BUT IT ADDS DEPTH OF FLAVOUR AND A SHARP PIQUANCY.

1. Heat the oil in a large frying pan (skillet) over a medium heat. Add the onion, red peppers, garlic and chilli and cook, stirring occasionally, for 5 minutes, or until tender. Stir in the ground spices and cook for 1 minute.
2. Add the tomatoes, tomato paste, ketchup and sugar and simmer for 10–15 minutes, or until the sauce starts to reduce and thicken. Season with salt and pepper and stir in half of the coriander.
3. Make 4 hollows in the sauce with the back of a spoon and break in the eggs, then cover the pan and simmer gently for 10 minutes, or until the eggs are cooked – the whites should be set and the yolks still slightly runny. Crumble the feta over the top and sprinkle with the remaining coriander.
4. Serve immediately with some warm pitta, flatbreads or challah bread to mop up the spicy tomato sauce.

2 tbsp olive oil
1 red onion, thinly sliced
3 garlic cloves, crushed
1 green (bell) pepper,
  deseeded and thinly sliced
1 red (bell) pepper, deseeded
  and thinly sliced
1 yellow (bell) pepper,
  deseeded and thinly sliced
1 tsp hot or smoked paprika
450g (1lb) ripe tomatoes,
  skinned and chopped
60ml (2fl oz/¼ cup) ketchup
a good pinch of sugar
8 medium free-range eggs
a handful of flat-leaf parsley,
  chopped
salt and freshly ground
  black pepper

VARIATIONS
- Use tinned tomatoes instead of fresh.
- Use only red peppers instead of a mixture.
- Substitute basil for parsley.
- Add a diced red chilli or a pinch of crushed dried chilli flakes.
- Add some crisp bacon or pancetta cubes.

VEGETARIAN

PIPERADE

THIS COLOURFUL DISH OF SCRAMBLED EGGS HAILS FROM THE BASQUE REGION IN SOUTHWEST FRANCE, CLOSE TO THE SPANISH BORDER. SERVE IT WITH SOME CRUSTY BREAD, TOASTED ENGLISH MUFFINS OR FRIED POTATOES.

1. Heat the oil in a large non-stick frying pan (skillet) set over a low heat. Add the onion, garlic and peppers and cook gently, stirring occasionally, for 10 minutes, or until really tender.
2. Stir in the paprika, tomatoes, ketchup and a good pinch of sugar and increase the heat to medium. Cook for 10 minutes, or until the sauce reduces and thickens. Season to taste with salt and pepper. Remove three-quarters of the mixture from the pan and keep warm.
3. Beat the eggs in a bowl with a little salt and pepper. Pour into the frying pan and stir gently into the remaining sauce with a wooden spoon over a low heat until the eggs start to set and scramble. Watch them carefully and don't overcook them – they should be creamy.
4. Gently stir the scrambled egg mixture into the reserved warm peppers and tomatoes. Add the parsley and divide between 4 serving plates. Serve immediately.

SPICED CORNED BEEF HASH

2 tbsp oil
1 large red onion, finely
  chopped
1 garlic clove, crushed
450g (1lb) cooked potatoes,
  cubed
1 × 350g (12oz) tin corned
  beef, roughly chopped
250g (9oz/1 cup) tinned
  sweetcorn kernels,
  drained
2 tbsp hot ketchup
a small handful of flat-leaf
  parsley, chopped
4 medium free-range eggs
salt and freshly grated black
  pepper
hot ketchup or hot sauce,
  for drizzling

CORNED BEEF HASH IS A REALLY TASTY BREAKFAST OR BRUNCH DISH. IT'S A GREAT SOURCE OF PROTEIN AND IS VERY FILLING, HELPING TO SUSTAIN YOU THROUGHOUT THE MORNING SO YOU DON'T NEED TO SNACK. PLUS IT'S A DELICIOUS WAY OF USING UP LEFTOVER BOILED OR ROAST POTATOES.

1. Heat the oil in a large frying pan (skillet) set over a medium heat. Add the onion and garlic and cook, stirring occasionally, for 5 minutes, or until softened.
2. Stir in the potatoes and cook, stirring occasionally, for 6–8 minutes, or until crisp and golden brown.
3. Add the corned beef, breaking up any lumps, with the sweetcorn and ketchup. Cook, stirring occasionally, for about 5 minutes, or until everything is heated through and starting to brown. Season with salt and pepper and add the parsley.
4. Reduce the heat to low and flatten the mixture by pressing down with a spatula. Make 4 hollows and break an egg into each one. Cover the pan with a lid or some foil and cook for 4–5 minutes, or until the egg whites are set but the yolks are still runny. If wished, flash under a hot grill (broiler) to brown the top of the hash and cook any film on top of the eggs.
5. Serve immediately, drizzled with ketchup or hot sauce.

TIP:
If you don't have hot ketchup or chilli ketchup, use regular instead together with a dash of hot sauce.

VARIATIONS
- Fry the eggs in another pan and serve on the side.
- Add some spinach or spring greens with the potatoes.
- Add some diced red (bell) pepper.
- To make the hash more spicy, add a dash of Tabasco.

SERVES 4
PREP 10 MINUTES
COOK 25–30 MINUTES

8 thin slices of bacon
450g (1lb) sausages
6 free-range medium eggs
4 tbsp milk or single (light)
   cream
3 tbsp finely chopped flat-
   leaf parsley or chives
100g (4oz/1 cup) grated
   Cheddar cheese
25g (1oz/2 tbsp) unsalted
   butter, plus extra for
   frying
4 large tortilla wraps
8 tbsp ketchup
2 ripe tomatoes, diced
salt and freshly ground
   black pepper

VARIATIONS
- Add some fried
  mushrooms, onions or
  red (bell) peppers.
- Use grated mozzarella
  instead of Cheddar.
- Drizzle with hot sauce
  or more ketchup.
- Use fried eggs instead
  of scrambled.

SAUSAGE, BACON AND EGG ROLL-UPS

THESE ROLL-UPS ARE PERFECT FOR A COOKED WEEKEND BREAKFAST OR BRUNCH. AND IF YOU PREFER NOT TO FRY THEM AT THE END YOU CAN JUST WARM AND FILL THE TORTILLAS, WRAP THEM IN FOIL AND EAT THEM ON THE GO.

1. Set a large non-stick frying pan (skillet) over a medium to high heat. When the pan is hot, add the bacon and cook for 3–4 minutes each side, or until the fat runs out and the bacon is golden brown and crispy. Remove from the pan and drain on kitchen paper (paper towels).
2. Add the sausages to the pan and cook in the bacon fat, turning occasionally, for 8–10 minutes, or until cooked right through and well browned. Remove and keep warm.
3. Whisk the eggs with the milk or cream and herbs in a bowl with half of the cheese. Season lightly with salt and pepper.
4. Melt the butter in a non-stick saucepan set over a low to medium heat and add the beaten egg mixture. Stir with a wooden spoon or spatula until the mixture is creamy and starts to set and scramble. Remove from the heat immediately.
5. Place the tortilla wraps on a clean work surface. Spread the ketchup over them and sprinkle with the diced tomatoes. Cut the sausages into thin slices and place on top with the bacon before adding the scrambled eggs and remaining cheese. Fold the sides of the tortillas over the filling and roll up.
6. Heat a knob of butter in a hot frying pan set over a medium to high heat. Add the rolled tortillas and cook for 1–2 minutes each side, until slightly crisp and golden brown. Serve immediately.

FULL ENGLISH TRAY BAKE

SERVES 4
PREP 10 MINUTES
COOK 15 MINUTES

olive oil, for brushing
400g (14oz) open field or
    chestnut mushrooms
8 slices of lean smoked
    back bacon
300g (10oz) cherry or baby
    plum tomatoes, halved
200g (7oz) baby spinach
    leaves
4 medium free-range eggs
100g (4oz/1 cup) grated
    Cheddar cheese
8 tbsp ketchup
salt and freshly ground
    black pepper

VARIATIONS

- Omit the bacon and
  add leftover diced
  cooked potatoes
  and cubed tofu for a
  veggie version.
- Add some sausages
  (pork, turkey or
  Quorn).
- Add some diced
  chorizo or use
  pancetta cubes
  instead of bacon.
- Sprinkle with crushed
  dried chilli flakes or
  chopped herbs.

THIS IS A REALLY EASY WAY TO PREPARE A NUTRITIOUS FAMILY BRUNCH. USING JUST ONE PAN MAKES YOUR LIFE EASIER AND THERE'S LESS WASHING-UP, TOO. IT'S A WIN WIN!

1. Preheat the oven to 200°C (180°C fan)/400°F/gas 6.
2. Lightly brush a large non-stick roasting pan with oil. Add the mushrooms, open-side down, bacon and tomatoes and bake for 10 minutes in the preheated oven.
3. Meanwhile, put the spinach leaves in a colander and pour some boiling water over them so they wilt and turn bright green. Pat dry with kitchen paper (paper towels) to remove any excess water.
4. Turn the mushrooms and bacon over and arrange little heaps of spinach in the pan around the tomatoes and mushrooms. Make 4 spaces between them and crack an egg into each one. Season with salt and pepper and sprinkle the grated cheese over the vegetables.
5. Bake in the oven for 5 minutes, or until the egg whites are set but the yolks are still runny and the cheese has melted.
6. Drizzle with the ketchup and serve immediately.

STARTERS

450g (1lb) frozen raw
   prawns (shrimp)
1 little gem or small cos
   (romaine) lettuce,
   shredded
lemon wedges, to serve

COCKTAIL SAUCE

120ml (4fl oz/½ cup)
   ketchup
2 tbsp tomato paste
1–2 tbsp horseradish
1 tsp red or white wine
   vinegar
a good squirt of lemon juice
a dash of hot sauce, e.g.
   Tabasco
a pinch of sweet paprika

VARIATIONS
- Add Worcestershire
  sauce, crushed garlic
  or diced gherkins (dill
  pickles).
- Add some garlic, chilli
  or onion powder.
- Add mayonnaise to
  the dressing for a
  Marie Rose sauce.
- Add some lobster or
  crayfish tail.

RETRO SHRIMP COCKTAIL

SHRIMP COCKTAIL USED TO BE ALL THE RAGE BACK
IN THE 1970S BUT THEN IT WENT OUT OF FASHION.
THANKFULLY, IT'S MAKING A COMEBACK AND TASTES
DELICIOUS IF YOU USE PLUMP, JUICY PRAWNS AND
DITCH THE ORIGINAL TASTELESS ICEBERG LETTUCE.
SERVE IN INDIVIDUAL GLASSES (AS OPPOSITE) OR
ARRANGE THE PRAWNS ON A PLATTER OF CRACKED
ICE ALONGSIDE THE COCKTAIL SAUCE IN A BOWL FOR
DIPPING.

1. Defrost the prawns in the fridge overnight.
2. Make the cocktail sauce: put all the ingredients in a bowl
   and stir until well blended and smooth, adjusting the
   horseradish and hot sauce to taste.
3. When the prawns have completely defrosted, drop them
   into a saucepan of boiling water for 2–3 minutes, or until
   they turn pink. Remove immediately with a slotted spoon
   and plunge them into a bowl of iced water.
4. Shell the prawns, leaving the tails on, and pat dry with
   kitchen paper (paper towels). Toss them in the cocktail
   sauce.
5. Divide the lettuce between 4 cocktail glasses or individual
   glass bowls. Top with the prawns and serve immediately
   with the lemon wedges.

BUFFALO WINGS

900g (2lb) chicken wings,
    cut in 2
oil, for brushing
1 tsp smoked paprika
4 tbsp ketchup
4 tbsp hot sauce
3 tbsp clear honey
60g (2oz/¼ cup) butter
salt and freshly ground
    black pepper

EVERYONE LOVES TANGY, STICKY BUFFALO WINGS. THEY MAKE THE PERFECT FINGER FOOD, BUFFET DISH, CANAPÉ OR PRE−DINNER APPETIZER. YOU CAN ALSO SERVE THEM FOR A LIGHT SUPPER WITH SOME BOILED OR STEAMED RICE AND A CRISP SALAD.

1. Preheat the oven to 200°C (180°C fan)/400°F/gas 6. Line a large baking tray (cookie sheet) with foil.
2. Brush the chicken wings with oil and season with salt and pepper. Arrange on a rack placed over the baking tray and bake in the preheated oven for 45 minutes, or until cooked through, golden brown and crisp.
3. Meanwhile, mix together the paprika, ketchup, hot sauce and honey. Grind in some black pepper and transfer to a small saucepan. Set over a low heat and stir in the butter. Cook gently for 5 minutes, or until the butter melts and the sauce thickens and reduces a little.
4. Coat the chicken wings in the hot sauce and return to the oven for 5 minutes, or until the wings are sticky, well glazed and a deep golden brown. Serve immediately while they are piping hot.

VARIATIONS
- Add some crushed garlic or lemon juice to the buffalo sauce.
- Use boned chicken thighs instead of wings.
- Serve with a blue cheese dip or tzatziki.

TIP:
For an even stickier, more caramelized finish, pop the coated buffalo wings under a hot grill (broiler) for 4−5 minutes.

CHEESY CHICKEN QUESADILLAS

SERVES 4
PREP 15 MINUTES
COOK 12–16 MINUTES

200g (7oz/2 cups) grated
  Cheddar cheese
6 spring onions (scallions),
  thinly sliced
1 fresh red chilli, diced
a handful of coriander
  (cilantro), chopped
1 ripe avocado, peeled,
  stoned (pitted) and diced
juice of 1 lime
225g (8oz) cooked chicken
  breast, shredded
2 tbsp ketchup
4 large flour tortilla wraps
olive oil, for brushing
salt and freshly ground
  black pepper
hot sauce or ketchup, for
  drizzling
Ketchup Pico de Gallo
  (see page 14) and soured
  cream, to serve

VARIATIONS

- Swap chicken for
  diced ham, chorizo,
  pancetta or bacon.
- For a vegetarian
  version, use tinned
  refried beans.
- Add tinned sweetcorn
  or kidney beans.

QUESADILLAS ARE VERY VERSATILE AND ARE GREAT AS STARTERS, TASTY SNACKS OR EVEN AS A LIGHT LUNCH OR SUPPER SERVED WITH SALAD OR GRIDDLED VEGETABLES.

1. In a bowl, mix together the cheese, spring onions, chilli and coriander. Season lightly with salt and pepper.
2. Sprinkle the avocado with the lime juice and add to the mixture with the chicken and ketchup. Stir gently and divide between 2 tortillas but not right up to the edges – leave a thin border around each one. Place the other tortillas on top and press firmly together.
3. Lightly brush a large non-stick frying pan (skillet) with oil and set over a medium heat. When it's really hot, add one of the quesadillas and cook for 3–4 minutes, or until crisp and golden underneath. Turn it over carefully and cook the other side until it's golden and the cheese melts. Slide out of the pan and keep warm while you cook the other quesadilla in the same way.
4. Cut each quesadilla into 6 wedges and serve drizzled with hot sauce or ketchup, some pico de gallo and soured cream.

TIP:

Alternatively, divide the filling between the 4 tortillas, spreading it over half, and then fold over to make a half-moon shape. Press down on the edges to seal before cooking as above.

4 tbsp olive oil
2 onions, thinly sliced
4 garlic cloves, crushed
1 large aubergine (eggplant), chopped
2 large courgettes (zucchini), sliced
2 red or green (bell) peppers, deseeded and sliced
450g (1lb) ripe tomatoes, skinned and chopped
60ml (2fl oz/¼ cup) ketchup
1 tsp sugar
a dash of red wine vinegar
¼ tsp crushed coriander seeds
a small handful of flat-leaf parsley or basil, chopped
salt and freshly ground black pepper
crusty bread or warm flatbreads, to serve

VARIATIONS
- Stir in some black olives or capers.
- Serve as a topping for bruschetta or crostini.
- Serve with griddled meat or chicken.

VEGAN

KETCHUP RATATOUILLE

THIS MEDITERRANEAN DISH OF STEWED VEGETABLES IS ONE OF THE SPECIALITIES OF NICE AND FEATURES THE DISTINCTIVE FLAVOURS, COLOURS AND INGREDIENTS OF PROVENCE. ADDING A LITTLE KETCHUP MAY BE ANATHEMA TO THE PURISTS BUT IT DOES ENHANCE THE FLAVOUR, MAKING IT FULLER AND MORE PIQUANT.

1. Heat the oil in a pan set over a low heat and add the onions and garlic. Cook, stirring occasionally, for 10 minutes, or until softened but not browned.
2. Add the aubergine, courgettes and peppers, then cover the pan and simmer for 15 minutes. Stir in the tomatoes, ketchup, sugar, vinegar and coriander seeds. Season with salt and pepper.
3. Cook gently over a low heat for 20–30 minutes, or until the vegetables are really tender and the mixture thickens and reduces. Sprinkle with parsley or basil and serve hot, lukewarm or cold with crusty bread or warm flatbreads.

MAKES ABOUT 20
PREP 15 MINUTES
STAND 15 MINUTES
COOK 5 MINUTES

450g (1lb) ripe tomatoes, diced
2 garlic cloves, crushed
a handful of fresh basil leaves, shredded
2 tbsp olive oil
1–2 tbsp ketchup
a few drops of balsamic vinegar
salt and freshly ground black pepper

GARLIC TOASTS
1 baguette (French stick)
3 garlic cloves, crushed
3 tbsp olive oil

VARIATIONS
- Add some diced roasted red (bell) pepper.
- Sprinkle the garlic toasts with grated cheese before baking.
- Use extra sweet baby plum or cherry tomatoes.

VEGAN

ITALIAN TOMATO AND BASIL BRUSCHETTA

BRUSCHETTA IS A GREAT APPETIZER FOR FAMILY GATHERINGS AND PARTIES, ESPECIALLY IN THE SUMMER. IT'S BEST EATEN FRESH WHILE THE TOASTS ARE STILL CRISP AND WARM.

1. Preheat the oven to 200°C (180°C fan)/400°F/gas 6. Line a baking tray (cookie sheet) with baking parchment.
2. Place the diced tomatoes in a sieve and drain off the juice. Transfer them to a bowl and stir in the garlic, basil and olive oil. Add ketchup and balsamic vinegar to taste and season with salt and pepper. Set aside for 15 minutes.
3. Meanwhile, make the garlic toasts: cut the baguette into slices, about 2cm (¾in) thick. Mix the garlic into the olive oil and brush over both sides of the bread slices. Place on the lined baking tray and bake in the preheated oven for about 5 minutes, or until crisp and golden brown.
4. Top the toasts with the tomato mixture and serve immediately.

CRISPY MASHED AVOCADO BASKETS

MAKES 12
PREP 15 MINUTES
COOK 8–10 MINUTES

olive oil, for brushing
12 wonton wrappers
1 large ripe avocado,
    peeled, stoned (pitted)
    and diced
juice of ½ lime
125g (4½oz/½ cup) Greek
    yoghurt
1–2 tbsp sweet chilli sauce
6 tbsp Ketchup Pico de
    Gallo (see page 14)
chopped coriander
    (cilantro), to garnish

THESE CRISPY MINI BASKETS CAN BE ENJOYED AS A PRETTY FIRST COURSE OR AS TASTY NIBBLES WITH PRE-DINNER DRINKS. YOU CAN COOK THE 'BASKETS' IN ADVANCE AND FILL THEM LATER JUST BEFORE SERVING. YOU CAN BUY WONTON WRAPPERS AT SOME LARGE SUPERMARKETS, ORIENTAL STORES AND DELIS OR ONLINE.

1. Preheat the oven to 200°C (180°C fan)/400°F/gas 6. Lightly brush a 12-hole mini muffin tin (pan) with oil.
2. Press a wonton wrapper down into each pan to make a basket shape, lining the base and sides. Bake in the preheated oven for 8–10 minutes until crisp and golden. Make sure that they do not over-brown. Leave to cool in the tin.
3. In a bowl, coarsely mash the avocado with the lime juice and stir in the yoghurt. Swirl the chilli sauce attractively through the mixture.
4. Divide between the cooled wonton baskets and then top with the pico de gallo. Sprinkle with coriander and serve.

TIP:
If you haven't got any Ketchup Pico de Gallo to hand, you can add 2 tablespoons ketchup to some shop-bought ready-made salsa.

SERVES 4–6
PREP 20 MINUTES
STAND 15 MINUTES
COOK 3–4 MINUTES

450g (1lb/1½ cups) fresh
   lump crab meat
juice of 1 lemon
12 asparagus spears,
   trimmed
1 large cos (romaine)
   lettuce, trimmed, washed
   and separated into leaves
2 hard-boiled free-range
   eggs, thickly sliced
12 baby plum or cherry
   tomatoes, halved
½ cucumber, thinly sliced
snipped chives, to garnish
salt and freshly ground
   black pepper

DRESSING
240g (8oz/1 cup)
   mayonnaise
3 tbsp ketchup
2 tbsp lemon juice
1 tbsp sweet pickle
1 tsp Dijon mustard
½ tsp horseradish relish
a dash of Worcestershire
   sauce
a dash of hot sauce, e.g.
   Tabasco
2 tbsp finely diced shallot
1 garlic clove, crushed

CRAB LOUIS SALAD

THIS CLASSIC CRAB SALAD SERVES SIX AS A STARTER OR FOUR AS A LIGHT LUNCH. USING REALLY FRESH, GOOD-QUALITY CRAB MEAT WILL MAKE ALL THE DIFFERENCE TO THIS DISH. THE AROMATIC, CREAMY SAUCE SHOULD HAVE A HINT OF HEAT AND SPICE AS WELL AS SWEETNESS FROM THE KETCHUP AND PICKLE.

1. Make the dressing: whisk the mayonnaise, lemon juice, ketchup, pickle, mustard and horseradish together in a bowl until smooth and well blended. Stir in the Worcestershire sauce and Tabasco to taste, then add the shallot and garlic. Cover and set aside for 15 minutes.
2. Mix the crab meat with the lemon juice and season lightly with salt and pepper.
3. Cook the asparagus spears in a saucepan of boiling salted water for 3–4 minutes, or until tender but still retain some 'bite' (al dente). Drain well and set aside to cool.
4. Arrange the lettuce leaves, eggs, tomatoes, cucumber and asparagus on the serving plates. Pile the crab meat in the centre and sprinkle with the chives. Let everyone help themselves to the dressing.

TIP: Don't chill the dressing in the fridge. It is best served at room temperature.

VARIATIONS
• Mix the crab meat into the dressing before serving.
• Add a few drops of wine vinegar to the dressing.
• Add some chilli powder or paprika to taste.
• Use red onion instead of a shallot.
• Add some radishes or avocado to the salad.

SERVES 4–6
PREP 20 MINUTES
CHILL 1 HOUR

450g (1lb) cooked prawns
(shrimp), peeled
1 red onion, diced
2 celery sticks, diced
½ cucumber, peeled and
diced
1 jalapeño, diced
400g (14oz/2 cups) diced
tomatoes (with juice)
120ml (4fl oz/½ cup)
ketchup
a bunch of coriander
(cilantro) chopped
360ml (12fl oz/1½ cups)
chilled tomato and clam
juice, e.g. Clamato
juice of 2 limes
1–2 tsp hot sauce, e.g.
Tabasco or Mexican
habanero sauce
½–1 tsp salt
1 avocado, peeled, stoned
(pitted) and diced
freshly ground black pepper
tortilla chips, to serve

MEXICAN SEAFOOD COCKTAIL

THIS DELICIOUS STARTER IS A HYBRID – SHRIMP COCKTAIL MEETS GAZPACHO. IT IS SERVED CHILLED AND IS PERFECT FOR SUMMER ENTERTAINING. IN MEXICO, IT IS SOMETIMES SERVED AS A HANGOVER CURE.

1. Cut three-quarters of the prawns in half and place in a large bowl with the onion, celery, cucumber, jalapeño, diced tomatoes and their juice, ketchup and coriander.
2. Add the tomato and clam juice, lime juice, hot sauce and salt to taste. Season with black pepper and stir in the avocado and remaining whole prawns.
3. Cover and chill in the fridge for at least 1 hour before serving in sundae glasses or glass bowls with some tortilla chips or salty crackers on the side.

TIP:
Many large supermarkets sell Clamato, a spicy tomato cocktail with clams. Or you can buy bottled clam juice and mix it with tomato juice.

VARIATIONS
- When tomatoes are out of season, use good-quality tinned ones instead.
- Add cooked squid, octopus, lump crab meat, clams, lobster or scallops.
- Use extra avocado and spring onions (scallions).

SOUPS & SALADS

SERVES 6
PREP 20 MINUTES
COOK 40 MINUTES

4 slices of back bacon
2 tbsp olive oil
1 large onion, finely
   chopped
2 celery sticks, diced
2 carrots, diced
1 red or green (bell) pepper,
   deseeded and diced
2 garlic cloves, crushed
2 × 300g (10oz) tins baby
   clams, drained and juice
   reserved
400ml (14fl oz/generous 1½
   cups) tinned clam juice
600ml (1 pint/2½ cups) fish
   stock
2 × 400g (14oz) tins
   chopped tomatoes
120ml (4fl oz/½ cup)
   ketchup
1 bay leaf
a few sprigs of fresh thyme
400g (14oz) potatoes,
   peeled and cut into large
   cubes
a dash of Tabasco
a handful of flat-leaf
   parsley, chopped
salt and freshly ground
   black pepper

MANHATTAN CLAM CHOWDER

WE'VE USED TINNED CLAMS BECAUSE THEY ARE MORE ACCESSIBLE THAN FRESH AND CAN BE KEPT IN YOUR KITCHEN CUPBOARD. THE TOMATOES AND KETCHUP ENHANCE THE FLAVOUR AND COLOUR OF THIS SOUP.

1. Cook the bacon in a large saucepan set over a medium heat, turning occasionally, for 4–5 minutes, or until it is golden brown and crispy. Remove and drain on kitchen paper (paper towels). Cut into small pieces and set aside.
2. Add the oil to the pan and cook the onion, celery, carrots, pepper and garlic, stirring occasionally, for 5 minutes, or until the vegetables are softened.
3. Return the bacon to the pan with the reserved clam juice, tinned clam juice, fish stock, tomatoes, ketchup and herbs. Bring to the boil, then reduce the heat and add the potatoes. Simmer gently for 20 minutes, or until the potatoes are tender and the liquid has reduced a little.
4. Stir in the clams and simmer for 5 minutes. Season to taste and add the Tabasco and most of the parsley. Remove the bay leaf and thyme sprigs.
5. Ladle the hot soup into bowls and serve immediately, sprinkled with the remaining parsley.

TIP:
Waxy potatoes work best in this recipe. Look for Maris Piper, Charlotte, Red Bliss and Yukon Gold.

VARIATIONS
• **Serve with crisp crackers, e.g. saltine or oyster.**
• **Add fresh clams in the last 10 minutes of cooking Cook until the shells open, discard any that stay shut.**

65

BLACK BEAN TORTILLA SOUP

SERVES 4
PREP 15 MINUTES
COOK 45–50 MINUTES

3 ripe large beefsteak
  tomatoes
2 tbsp olive oil
1 large onion, chopped
3 garlic cloves, crushed
1 tsp chilli powder
60ml (2fl oz/¼ cup) ketchup
a handful of coriander
  (cilantro), chopped
1 × 400g (14oz) tin black
  beans, rinsed and drained
900ml (1½ pints/3¾ cups)
  hot vegetable stock
a pinch of soft brown sugar
4 tbsp soured cream
salt and freshly ground
  black pepper
lime wedges, to serve

TOPPING

75g (3oz) tortilla chips,
  roughly crushed
1 ripe small avocado,
  peeled, stoned (pitted)
  and diced
1 red chilli, deseeded and
  shredded
50g (2oz/½ cup) grated
  Cheddar or Monterey
  Jack cheese

THIS SPICY TEX-MEX SOUP IS SURPRISINGLY FILLING AND LOOKS SO PRETTY TOPPED WITH TORTILLA CHIPS, AVOCADO, CHILLI AND CHEESE. YOU CAN MAKE IT IN ADVANCE TO REHEAT THE FOLLOWING DAY, AND PREPARE THE TOPPING JUST BEFORE SERVING IT.

1. Preheat the grill (broiler). Line a grill pan with foil and place the tomatoes in it. Cook under the hot grill for 12–15 minutes, turning occasionally, until softened and charred all over. Remove and discard the skins, and chop coarsely.
2. Heat the oil in a saucepan set over a low to medium heat. Cook the onion and garlic, stirring occasionally, for 10 minutes, or until softened.
3. Stir in the chilli powder and cook for 1 minute. Add the tomatoes, ketchup, coriander and three-quarters of the beans (reserving the rest) together with the stock. Bring to the boil, then reduce the heat and simmer gently for 15–20 minutes. Stir in the sugar and season to taste.
4. Blitz the soup in a blender or food processor until smooth. Return to the pan, add the reserved black beans and heat through gently.
5. Ladle the hot soup into 4 shallow bowls and swirl in the soured cream. Top with the tortilla chips, avocado, chilli and grated cheese. Serve hot with lime wedges.

VARIATIONS
- Use 8 ripe vine tomatoes instead of beefsteak tomatoes.
- Substitute Greek yoghurt for the soured cream.
- Sprinkle with chopped coriander or fresh basil.
- Use red kidney beans instead of black beans.
- Add a dash of hot sauce, e.g. Tabasco.

SERVES 4–6
PREP 20 MINUTES
SOAK 15–20 MINUTES
CHILL 2 HOURS

250g (9oz/5 cups) stale
   white breadcrumbs
900g (1lb) ripe tomatoes,
   skinned and chopped
2 red or green (bell)
   peppers, deseeded and
   chopped
3 garlic cloves, crushed
1 cucumber, peeled and
   chopped
5 tbsp fruity green olive oil
4 tbsp sherry vinegar
2 tbsp ketchup
600ml (1 pint/2½ cups) cold
   water
salt and freshly ground
   black pepper
ice cubes, to serve

GARNISHES

diced spring onions
   (scallions), cucumber,
   red or green peppers,
   chopped parsley or mint,
   crispy bread croûtons,
   diced black olives, cubed
   ham or chorizo, chopped
   hard-boiled egg

KETCHUP GAZPACHO

THIS CHILLED TOMATO SOUP FROM ANDALUSIA IN
SOUTHERN SPAIN TASTES REMARKABLY LIKE A LIQUID
SALAD! ADDING KETCHUP GIVES IT A KICK TASTE-WISE
AND ENHANCES THE FLAVOUR. IT'S THE PERFECT WAY
TO COOL DOWN ON A HOT SUMMER'S DAY.

1. Put the breadcrumbs in a bowl, add just enough cold water
   to cover them and leave to soak for 15–20 minutes, or until
   the water has been absorbed.
2. Place the soaked breadcrumbs in a blender with the
   tomatoes, peppers, garlic, cucumber, olive oil, vinegar and
   ketchup. Add a little water and blitz until smooth. Keep
   adding the water and blitzing until you have the desired
   consistency – you may not want to add it all if you want to
   end up with a thicker soup.
3. Pour into a bowl, then cover and chill in the fridge for at
   least 2 hours. Before serving, check the seasoning, adding
   salt and pepper to taste and more vinegar, if necessary.
4. When you're ready to serve, ladle the soup into shallow
   bowls and add ice cubes to each. If it's too thick, thin with
   iced water. Let everyone add garnishes of their choice.

TIP:

Brush some sliced crusty white bread with a cut garlic clove
and some olive oil and toast in a ridged griddle pan until
golden and crisp. Serve with the gazpacho.

VARIATIONS

- Use cold vegetable or chicken stock instead of water.
- Add sweet red onion – not too much, the soup is raw.
- For a more liquid soup, add more water or stock.

1kg (2lb 4oz) live mussels (shells on)
2 tbsp olive oil
1 large red onion, finely chopped
1 large leek, chopped
3 garlic cloves, crushed
1 red chilli, deseeded and diced
2 × 400g (14oz) tins chopped tomatoes
600ml (1 pint/2½ cups) hot fish stock
60ml (4floz/¼ cup) ketchup
a handful of flat-leaf parsley, chopped
salt and freshly ground black pepper
crusty bread, to serve

VARIATIONS

- Use chopped basil or coriander (cilantro) instead of parsley.
- Stir a little green pesto into each bowl.
- If you don't have fish stock, use vegetable instead.
- Make the soup with fresh clams instead of mussels.

ITALIAN TOMATO AND MUSSEL SOUP

THIS SOUP IS VERY FILLING AND PACKED WITH LEAN PROTEIN FROM THE MUSSELS. IT'S EASY TO PREPARE AND COOK FRESH MUSSELS SAFELY AS LONG AS YOU FOLLOW THE INSTRUCTIONS IN THE METHOD BELOW AND DISCARD ANY THAT ARE OPEN BEFORE COOKING OR FAIL TO OPEN AFTERWARDS.

1. Put the mussels into a large bowl of cold water and discard any that are open or cracked. Scrub the rest under running cold water and scrape away the wispy 'beards'.
2. Heat the oil in a pan set over a low to medium heat and cook the onion, leek, garlic and chilli, stirring occasionally, for 8–10 minutes, or until softened but not browned.
3. Add the tomatoes, stock and ketchup and bring to the boil. Cook for 1 minute, then reduce the heat to low, cover the pan and simmer gently for 10–15 minutes.
4. Meanwhile, cook the mussels. Tip into a large heavy-based saucepan, add a tablespoon of water and cover. Cook over a high heat, shaking gently occasionally, for 3–4 minutes, or until the shells open. Drain in a colander over a bowl to catch any juices. Throw away any mussels that fail to open.
5. Pour the mussel juice through a sieve into the soup. Remove three-quarters of the mussels from their shells (reserving the rest for the garnish) and stir them gently into the soup. Season to taste with salt and pepper, and simmer gently for 5 minutes. Stir in the parsley.
6. Ladle the soup into 4 serving bowls and add the reserved mussels in their shells. Serve immediately with crusty bread.

TIP:
Provide a large plate for all the mussel shells.

SERVES 4
PREP 15 MINUTES
COOK 50-60 MINUTES

1kg (2lb 4oz) juicy ripe
  tomatoes, halved
2 large red onions, sliced
3 garlic cloves, left whole
  and unpeeled
2 carrots, sliced
1 tsp sugar
3-4 tbsp olive oil
2 tsp smoked paprika
3 tbsp ketchup
900ml (1½ pints/3¾ cups)
  hot vegetable stock
2-3 drops red wine vinegar
4 heaped tsp crème fraîche
4 tsp basil oil (optional)
4 sprigs of basil
salt and freshly ground
  black pepper
sourdough or crusty bread,
  to serve

VARIATIONS
- Roast 2 red (bell)
  peppers with the
  other vegetables.
- Top with fried bacon
  lardons.
- Use balsamic instead
  of red wine vinegar.
- Add a dash of
  Worcestershire sauce
  or soy sauce.

VEGETARIAN

SMOKY PAPRIKA ROASTED TOMATO SOUP

THE COMBINATION OF SMOKED PAPRIKA AND ROASTING THE VEGETABLES UNTIL THEY ARE SLIGHTLY CHARRED GIVES THIS SOUP ITS DISTINCTIVE SMOKY TASTE. IT IS NATURALLY QUITE SWEET BUT THE KETCHUP AND RED WINE VINEGAR ADD A SHARP, TANGY EDGE.

1. Preheat the oven to 190°C (170°C fan)/375°F/gas 5.
2. Put the tomatoes, cut-side up, in a roasting pan with the onions, garlic and carrots. Sprinkle with the sugar, drizzle with the olive oil and season with salt and pepper.
3. Roast in the preheated oven for 45 minutes, or until the vegetables are tender and starting to char around the edges. Check them from time to time, turning the onions and carrots in the oil to prevent them sticking.
4. Remove the garlic cloves and squeeze out the garlic into a large saucepan, discarding the skins. Add all the roasted vegetables and any remaining oil and set over a medium heat. Stir in the smoked paprika, cook for 1 minute and then add the ketchup and the hot stock. Bring to the boil, then reduce the heat to medium and cook for 5-10 minutes.
5. Blitz the soup in batches in a blender or food processor until smooth. Return to the pan, stir in the vinegar and reheat gently.
6. Ladle the hot soup into bowls and swirl in the crème fraîche and basil oil (if using). Garnish with a sprig of basil and serve with bread.

4 × 100g (4oz) chicken
  breast fillets (skin on)
120ml (4fl oz/½ cup)
  Barbecue Sauce (see page
  16)
2 large sweet potatoes,
  peeled and cut into
  chunks
2 red onions, cut into
  wedges
2 red or yellow (bell)
  peppers, deseeded and
  sliced
3 tbsp olive oil
150g (5oz) mixed salad
  leaves
25g (1oz/¼ cup) toasted
  pine nuts
salt and freshly ground
  black pepper
ketchup, to serve (optional)

DRESSING

3 tbsp olive oil
1 tbsp wine vinegar
juice of 1 lemon
1 garlic clove, crushed
1 tsp grated fresh root
  ginger
1 tsp honey mustard

BBQ CHICKEN SALAD

THIS CHICKEN TASTES FABULOUS, COOKED OVER HOT COALS ON THE BARBECUE UNTIL IT'S CRISP, CHARRED AND SMOKY ON THE OUTSIDE, AND JUICY AND SUCCULENT ON THE INSIDE. YOU COULD GRILL THE VEGETABLES IN SOME FOIL ON THE BARBECUE, TOO.

1. Put the chicken into a large container and pour over the barbecue sauce. Turn in the sauce until coated all over. Cover and chill in the fridge for at least 30 minutes.
2. Meanwhile, preheat the oven to 200°C (180°C fan)/400°F/ gas 6. Light the barbecue.
3. Put the sweet potatoes, red onions and peppers into a roasting pan. Drizzle with olive oil and season with salt and pepper. Roast in the preheated oven for 25–30 minutes, turning once or twice, until tender and golden brown.
4. Meanwhile, cook the chicken over hot coals on the barbecue, turning it once or twice and basting with any leftover sauce, for 15 minutes, or until crisp and brown and cooked right through. When you insert a skewer, the juices should run clear. Place on a wooden board and cut into slices.
5. Blitz all the dressing ingredients in a blender until smooth, or shake them together in a screw-top jar.
6. Put the roasted vegetables and salad leaves in a large bowl and toss with the dressing. Divide between 4 serving plates and sprinkle with pine nuts. Lay the chicken on top and serve immediately with ketchup on the side, if desired.

VARIATIONS
- Use squash, beetroot (beets) or carrots instead of sweet potato.
- Drizzle balsamic vinegar over just before serving.
- Use chicken thighs or wings instead of breasts.

71

ITALIAN TRICOLORE PASTA SALAD

SERVES 4
PREP 15 MINUTES
COOK 10 MINUTES

300g (7oz) pasta shapes, e.g. orecchiette, fusilli, farfalle (dried weight)
200g (7oz) cherry or baby plum tomatoes, halved or quartered
150g (5oz) mini mozzarella balls (bocconcini)
90ml (3fl oz/⅓ cup) Ketchup Vinaigrette (see page 19)
1 ripe avocado, peeled, stoned (pitted) and cubed
a few fresh basil leaves, torn or shredded
salt and freshly ground black pepper

THIS COLOURFUL AND REFRESHING SALAD IS PERFECT FOR SUMMER GATHERINGS. THE PASTA IS TOSSED WITH CREAMY AVOCADO AND THE TRADITIONAL INGREDIENTS FOR A CAPRESE SALAD – THE COLOURS OF THE ITALIAN FLAG.

1. Cook the pasta according to the instructions on the packet. Drain well and rinse under running cold water, then drain again.
2. Put the pasta in a serving bowl with the tomatoes and mozzarella balls and stir gently to distribute the tomatoes throughout the pasta.
3. Toss lightly in the vinaigrette and then stir in the avocado and basil. Check the seasoning, adding salt and pepper, to taste.

VARIATIONS
- Substitute feta cubes for the mozzarella.
- Add some baby spinach leaves instead of avocado.
- Add drained and thinly sliced bottled red or yellow (bell) peppers.
- Add some drained artichoke hearts or capers.

VEGGIE MEXICAN TACO SALAD

SERVES 4
PREP 20 MINUTES

1 cos (romaine) lettuce, trimmed and chopped into pieces

300g (10oz) baby plum or cherry tomatoes, halved

1 × 400g (14oz) tin black beans, drained rinsed

a bunch of spring onions (scallions), thinly sliced

1 jalapeño, diced

1 ripe avocado, peeled, stoned (pitted) and diced

juice of 1 lime

a handful of fresh coriander (cilantro), chopped

75g (3oz/¾ cup) grated Cheddar cheese

120ml (4fl oz/½ cup) Ketchup Pico de Gallo (see page 14)

90ml (3fl oz/scant ½ cup) soured cream

100g (4oz) tortilla chips, lightly crumbled

TIP:

Don't crush the tortilla chips too much. Break each one into 3 or 4 pieces.

A CLASSIC TACO SALAD IS MADE WITH LEAN MINCED (GROUND) BEEF OR TURKEY BUT WE'VE USED BLACK BEANS INSTEAD IN THIS HEALTHY VEGETARIAN VERSION. EVEN PEOPLE – INCLUDING CHILDREN – WHO PROFESS NOT TO LIKE SALAD WILL LOVE THIS.

1. Put the lettuce, tomatoes, black beans, spring onions and jalapeño in a large bowl and mix together.
2. Toss the avocado in the lime juice and add to the salad in the bowl with the coriander and grated cheese.
3. Mix the pico de gallo and soured cream in a small bowl and use as a dressing. Either drizzle it over the top of the salad or lightly toss through it.
4. Crumble the tortilla chips over the top (see Tip) and serve immediately.

VARIATIONS

- Add some tinned or fresh sweetcorn kernels.
- Mix in some diced red, green or yellow (bell) pepper.
- Use diced red onion instead of spring onions.
- Add some diced cucumber or gherkins (dill pickles).
- Use guacamole or Greek yoghurt instead of soured cream.
- Use red kidney beans instead of black ones.
- Use a fresh red chilli instead of the jalapeño.

LIGHT MEALS

VEGAN TLT SANDWICH

SERVES 4
PREP 15 MINUTES
COOK 4–8 MINUTES

400g (14oz) extra-firm tofu
2 tbsp cornflour
   (cornstarch)
2 tbsp sunflower oil
8 slices whole-grain or
   multi-seed bread
1 ripe avocado, peeled,
   stoned (pitted) and
   mashed
4 tbsp vegan mayo
2 tbsp ketchup
2 ripe tomatoes, sliced
a few crisp cos (romaine) or
   iceberg lettuce leaves
salt and freshly ground
   black pepper

VARIATIONS
- Add some roasted
  vegetables.
- Use hot or chilli
  ketchup.
- Instead of lettuce, try
  wild rocket (arugula)
  or watercress.
- Use warm split pitta
  breads or wraps
  instead of toasted
  bread.

THIS DELICIOUS VEGAN VERSION OF A BLT (BACON, LETTUCE AND TOMATO) SANDWICH IS MADE WITH CRISP FRIED TOFU. IT'S HEALTHY AND NUTRITIOUS AND PACKED WITH PLANT PROTEIN. WHAT'S NOT TO LIKE?

1. Cut the tofu into slices and lightly dust them with cornflour. Season with salt and pepper.
2. Heat the oil in a frying pan (skillet) set over a medium heat and fry the tofu, a few slices at a time in batches, for 1–2 minutes each side, or until crisp and golden. Remove with a slotted spoon and drain on kitchen paper (paper towels).
3. Meanwhile, lightly toast the bread and spread 4 slices with the mashed avocado. Mix the vegan mayo and ketchup together and spread over the remaining slices.
4. Cover the avocado with the sliced tomatoes and top with the hot fried tofu. Add a layer of lettuce and cover with the remaining mayo-spread toast slices. Cut the sandwiches in half or into quarters and serve straight away while the tofu is still hot.

SERVES 4
PREP 20 MINUTES
COOK 20 MINUTES

olive oil, for brushing
2 × 400g (14oz) tins green
   jackfruit in brine, drained
120ml (4fl oz/½ cup)
   Barbecue Sauce (see page
   16)
4 pitta breads
1 large ripe avocado,
   peeled, stoned (pitted)
   and mashed
2 ripe tomatoes, thinly
   sliced

COLESLAW

¼ red cabbage, cored and
   thinly shredded
½ red onion, grated
2 carrots, grated
4 tbsp mayonnaise
1 tbsp ketchup
1 tsp Dijon mustard
a handful of flat-leaf
   parsley, finely chopped
50g (2oz/½ cup) chopped
   walnuts or pecans
a squeeze of lemon juice

VEGAN

PULLED BBQ JACKFRUIT PITTAS

JACKFRUIT HAS BECOME A GREAT VEGGIE SUBSTITUTE FOR MEAT, AND IT WORKS REALLY WELL AS A FILLING FOR PITTAS WITH TANGY BARBECUE SAUCE. USING FORKS TO SHRED IT GIVES IT THE TEXTURE OF PULLED PORK.

1. Preheat the oven to 200°C (180°C fan)/400°F/gas 6. Line a baking tray (cookie sheet) with foil and brush with olive oil.
2. Squeeze any liquid out of the jackfruit pieces and pat dry with kitchen paper (paper towels). Shred them with 2 forks and transfer to a bowl. Add the barbecue sauce and mix until all the jackfruit strands are coated.
3. Spread the jackfruit out in a single layer on the lined baking tray and bake in the preheated oven for 20 minutes, or until the jackfruit is crisp and browned.
4. Meanwhile, make the coleslaw: mix the cabbage, onion and carrots with the mayonnaise, ketchup and mustard. When everything is lightly coated, stir in the parsley, nuts and lemon juice.
5. Lightly toast or warm the pitta breads and split each one along the side to open it up and form a 'pocket'. Fill with the mashed avocado and tomato slices, and then add the jackfruit and coleslaw. Serve immediately.

VARIATIONS
- Use shop-bought coleslaw or tzatziki.
- Use as a filling for wraps, soft bread rolls or mini baguettes (French sticks).
- Add lettuce, spring onions (scallions) and cucumber.

BAKED SWEET POTATO JACKETS AND KETCHUP CHILI

SERVES 4
PREP 15 MINUTES
COOK 45 MINUTES

2 tbsp olive oil, plus extra for rubbing
4 medium sweet potatoes, washed and scrubbed
1 large red onion, diced
2 garlic cloves, crushed
1 red (bell) pepper, deseeded and diced
1–2 tsp chilli powder
1 × 400g (14oz) tin chopped tomatoes
60ml (2fl oz/¼ cup) ketchup
1 × 400g (14oz) tin red kidney beans, drained and rinsed
a few sprigs of coriander (cilantro), chopped
100g (4oz/1 cup) grated Cheddar cheese
salt and freshly ground black pepper
soured cream and Ketchup Pico de Gallo (see page 14), to serve (optional)

VARIATIONS
- Use black beans instead of red kidney beans.
- Top the baked sweet potatoes with minced (ground) beef chili.

ADDING KETCHUP TO VEGETARIAN CHILI MAKES IT REALLY TASTY AND LIVENS IT UP. IT'S EASY TO MAKE AND WILL COOK AWAY WHILE THE SWEET POTATOES ARE BAKING IN THE OVEN.

1. Preheat the oven to 190°C (170°C fan)/375°F/gas 5.
2. Rub a little olive oil over the sweet potatoes and place on a baking tray (cookie sheet). Bake in the preheated oven for 45 minutes, or until tender when you press them gently.
3. Meanwhile, heat the oil in a saucepan set over a low to medium heat. Add the onion, garlic and red pepper and cook, stirring occasionally, for 6–8 minutes until tender but not browned.
4. Stir in the chilli powder and cook for 1 minute. Add the tomatoes, ketchup and kidney beans and simmer gently for 10–15 minutes, or until reduced and thickened. Stir in the coriander and season to taste with salt and pepper.
5. Cut a cross in the top of each sweet potato and press gently on the sides to open it up. Place one on each serving plate and spoon the chili over the top. Sprinkle with grated Cheddar and serve with soured cream and ketchup pico de gallo (if wished).

TIP:
Vegans can use non-dairy shredded vegan cheese.

400g (14oz) lean sirloin or
    rump steaks, fat removed
120ml (4fl oz/½ cup)
    Barbecue Sauce (see page
    16)
2 carrots, cut into thin
    matchsticks
4 radishes, thinly sliced
1 red (bell) pepper, deseeded
    and thinly sliced
1 small ridged cucumber,
    thinly sliced
4 tbsp rice vinegar
4 tbsp caster (superfine)
    sugar
1 tbsp nam pla (Thai fish
    sauce)
olive oil, for brushing
4 small baguettes (French
    sticks), halved, hollowed
chopped coriander (cilantro),
    to garnish

RED-HOT MAYO

120g (4oz/½ cup) mayonnaise
2 spring onions (scallions),
    diced
2 tbsp sweet chilli sauce or
    sriracha
1–2 tsp ketchup

BBQ STEAK BANH-MI

THE KETCHUP IN THE BARBECUE SAUCE AND MAYO COMPLEMENTS THE VIETNAMESE FLAVOURS IN THIS SPICY STEAK BAGUETTE. OF COURSE, FOR A REALLY SMOKY TASTE YOU COULD COOK THE STEAK OVER HOT COALS ON AN OUTDOOR GRILL OR BARBECUE.

1. Make the red-hot mayo: mix all the ingredients together in a bowl. Cover and chill in the fridge until you're ready to assemble the baguettes.
2. Put the steaks in a bowl and pour the barbecue sauce over them. Turn them in the sauce until they are completely coated and marinate in a cool place for 1 hour.
3. Mix together the carrots, radishes, pepper and cucumber in a glass bowl. Heat the vinegar and sugar in a small saucepan, stirring until the sugar dissolves, then bring to the boil. Remove from the heat and stir in the nam pla. Pour over the vegetables and leave for 1 hour or longer.
4. Lightly oil a large frying pan (skillet) or ridged griddle pan. Place over a medium to high heat, then cook the steaks for 2–4 minutes each side, depending on how rare or well done you like them. Remove and cut into thin slices.
5. Split the baguettes in half lengthways and scoop out some soft bread in the centre to leave a crusty shell. Spread the red-hot mayo over the bases and then add the sliced steak. Top with the carrot and radish mixture, then sprinkle with coriander. Cover with the baguette tops, pressing down firmly. Eat immediately while the steak is still hot.

VARIATIONS
- Use grilled (broiled) chicken or tofu instead of steak.
- Add some pickled chillies or jalapeños.
- Add some thinly sliced red onion.

STICKY SAUSAGE HOT DOGS

SERVES 4
PREP 10 MINUTES
COOK 20 MINUTES

spray oil
8 pork sausages
2 red onions, thinly sliced
1 tsp black mustard seeds
1 tbsp balsamic vinegar
4 sub rolls or hot dog rolls
4 tbsp ketchup
salt and freshly ground
   black pepper

STICKY GLAZE

2 tbsp clear honey
1 tbsp ketchup
1 tbsp balsamic vinegar
1 tsp Dijon mustard

VARIATIONS

- Use this as a filling for split pitta breads or for wraps.
- Vegetarians can use Quorn or vegan sausages.
- Serve with mustard or some fruity relish or chutney.

THESE SAUSAGES ARE DELICIOUSLY SWEET, AROMATIC AND STICKY – MUCH MORE FLAVOURFUL AND INTERESTING THAN THE USUAL FRANKFURTERS. THEY ARE PERFECT FOR BONFIRE PARTIES AND HALLOWEEN.

1. Preheat the oven to 200°C (180°C fan)/400°F/gas 6.
2. Lightly spray a roasting pan with oil and place in the hot oven for 5 minutes to warm it up. Place the sausages in the hot pan and cook for 5 minutes until browned underneath.
3. Turn them over and add the onions and mustard seeds to the pan. Sprinkle the onions with the balsamic vinegar and season with salt and pepper. Return to the oven for 5 minutes, turning the sausages once or twice.
4. Mix together the ingredients for the sticky glaze and brush over the sausages. Cook in the oven for a further 10 minutes, or until the sausages are browned, sticky and thoroughly cooked and the onions are golden and tender.
5. Split and lightly toast the bread rolls or warm them in a ridged griddle pan. Spread the base of each roll with ketchup and cover with the sausages and onions. Top with the other halves of the rolls and enjoy.

SERVES 4
PREP 15 MINUTES
COOK 25–35 MINUTES

2 tbsp olive oil, plus extra
  for brushing
2 red onions, thinly sliced
2 red or green (bell)
  peppers, deseeded and
  sliced
2 tsp balsamic vinegar
1 tsp sugar
450g (1lb) lean rump, sirloin
  or rib-eye steak, visible
  fat removed
a dash of Worcestershire
  sauce
4 tbsp ketchup
1 tbsp mayonnaise
4 mini baguettes (French
  sticks) or sub rolls
8 thin slices of Provolone
  cheese
salt and freshly ground
  black pepper
mustard, to serve

VARIATIONS
- Use sliced mozzarella,
  Cheddar, Monterey
  Jack or Swiss cheese.
- Cook some
  mushrooms with the
  onions and peppers.
- Add some chopped
  parsley.

PHILLY CHEESE STEAK TOASTIE

THIS TOASTED CHEESE AND STEAK SANDWICH IS AN AMERICAN CLASSIC AND MAKES A FILLING LUNCH. WE'VE MADE A KETCHUP MAYO TO SPREAD OVER THE ROLLS AND ADD EXTRA FLAVOUR.

1. Heat the olive oil in a frying pan (skillet) set over a low to medium heat. Add the onions and peppers and cook, stirring occasionally, for 10–15 minutes, or until they are softened and the onions are golden brown and starting to caramelize. Stir in the vinegar and sugar and season with salt and pepper.
2. Lightly brush a clean large frying pan or ridged griddle pan with oil. Set over a medium to high heat and, when it's hot, add the steaks. Cook for 2–4 minutes each side, depending on how rare or well done you like them. Remove from the pan and let them rest for 2–3 minutes before cutting into really thin slices. Sprinkle with a dash of Worcestershire sauce.
3. Mix the ketchup with the mayonnaise. Cut the rolls in half and spread both sides with the ketchup mayo. Place a slice of cheese on both sides and divide the onions and peppers between them. Top with the sliced steak, then cover with the top halves of the rolls and press down firmly.
4. Set a cast-iron pan or ridged griddle pan over a medium heat and, when it's hot, add the rolls. Cook for 3–4 minutes each side until warm and crispy and the cheese starts to melt. Serve immediately with mustard on the side.

BAKED GEMISTA

SERVES 4
PREP 15 MINUTES
STAND 1 HOUR
COOK 35–45 MINUTES

4 large ripe beefsteak
   tomatoes with stems
4 handfuls of Arborio risotto
   rice
3 tbsp ketchup
2 tbsp fruity green olive oil
a handful of dill, finely
   chopped
2 garlic cloves, crushed
50g (2oz/½ cup) toasted
   pine nuts
4 large fresh basil leaves
salt and freshly ground
   black pepper

VARIATIONS
- Use chopped flat-leaf
  parsley, mint or basil
  instead of dill.
- Add some crushed
  dried chilli flakes,
  currants or capers.
- Squeeze some lemon
  juice over the rice
  stuffing before
  cooking.

STUFFED TOMATOES ARE A POPULAR SUMMER DISH THROUGHOUT GREECE AND ARE SERVED AT HOME AS WELL AS IN TAVERNAS. TOMATO PASTE IS USUALLY USED BUT WE HAVE SUBSTITUTED KETCHUP. EAT AS A LIGHT LUNCH OR AS A SIDE DISH. GEMISTA WILL KEEP WELL IN THE FRIDGE FOR UP TO 2 DAYS.

1. Cut the tops off the tomatoes to make 'lids'. With a teaspoon or a melon scooper, scoop out all the seeds, pulp and juices into a bowl. Stand the scooped-out tomato 'shells' in a deep ovenproof dish and keep the lids.
2. Add the rice to the bowl of tomato pulp, a handful at a time, and stir in. Add the ketchup and olive oil and season with plenty of salt and pepper. Set aside to stand for 1 hour.
3. When the rice has absorbed most of the liquid it's ready. Stir in the dill, garlic and pine nuts. Preheat the oven to 180°C (160°C fan)/350°F/gas 4.
4. Season the tomato shells with salt and pepper and place a basil leaf in the bottom of each one. Divide the rice mixture between the tomatoes and place the lids on top. Drizzle with some olive oil, then pour enough water into the dish around the tomatoes to come up to a depth of 1cm (½in).
5. Bake in the preheated oven for 35–45 minutes, or until the tomatoes are cooked but not collapsing and the rice is tender. Serve lukewarm or cold.

TIP:
For the best flavour, use locally grown, sun-ripened tomatoes.

SERVES 4
PREP 10 MINUTES
COOK 6 MINUTES

120g (4oz/½ cup)
  mayonnaise
60ml (2fl oz/¼ cup) ketchup
1 tbsp horseradish relish or
  sauce
50g (2oz/4 tbsp) unsalted
  butter, at room
  temperature
8 slices of rye bread
4 slices of Swiss cheese,
  e.g. Emmenthal
4 gherkins (dill pickles),
  sliced
350g (12oz) sliced pastrami
175g (6oz/1 cup) sauerkraut,
  drained and rinsed
4 tsp mustard
potato crisps (potato chips)
  and ketchup, to serve

VARIATIONS

- Use coleslaw instead
  of sauerkraut.
- Use hot ketchup
  or add a dash
  of hot sauce or
  Worcestershire sauce.
- Add 1 tbsp sweet
  pickle to the ketchup
  mayo.
- Use corned beef or
  even ham instead of
  pastrami.

TOASTED CHEESY PASTRAMI REUBENS

A CLASSIC DELI REUBEN IS MADE WITH CORNED BEEF BUT WE'VE USED PASTRAMI INSTEAD. DON'T BE PUT OFF IF YOU DON'T OWN A SANDWICH MAKER (PRESS) – THESE LOADED TOASTIES TASTE JUST AS GOOD COOKED IN A FRYING PAN.

1. In a bowl, mix together the mayonnaise, ketchup and horseradish.
2. Thinly spread the butter over each slice of bread. Turn the bread over and spread the ketchup mayo over 4 slices. Add the cheese, sliced gherkins and pastrami, and then top with the sauerkraut.
3. Thinly spread the mustard over the remaining bread and use to cover the sandwiches (with the buttered side on the outside).
4. Place a large frying pan (skillet) over a medium heat and when it's hot, add the sandwiches to the pan (if necessary do this in batches – two at a time). Cook for 3 minutes each side, or until the cheese melts and the bread is toasted. Alternatively, cook in a sandwich maker (sandwich or panini press).
5. Cut each sandwich in half diagonally and serve immediately with potato crisps and ketchup.

TIP:
You can buy sauerkraut in cans or jars in most supermarkets.

SERVES 4
PREP 15 MINUTES
CHILL 1 HOUR
COOK 6–8 MINUTES

60g (2oz/¼ cup)
  mayonnaise
1 large free-range egg,
  beaten
2 tsp Dijon mustard
1 tsp Worcestershire sauce
1 tsp lemon juice
1 tsp Old Bay seasoning
  (optional)
500g (1lb 2oz) white lump
  crab meat
a few sprigs of flat-leaf
  parsley, finely chopped
50g (2oz/½ cup) fresh white
  breadcrumbs
3 tbsp olive oil
salt and freshly ground
  black pepper
lemon wedges, to serve

COCKTAIL SAUCE

240ml (8fl oz/1 cup)
  ketchup
3 tbsp horseradish sauce
2–3 tsp Worcestershire
  sauce
juice of ½ lemon
a dash of hot sauce

TIP:

Bake the cakes in an oven at
230°C (210°C fan)/450°F/gas
8 for 12 minutes.

MARYLAND CRAB CAKES

IT'S BEST TO USE FRESH GOOD-QUALITY CRAB MEAT TO MAKE THESE SIMPLE CRAB CAKES BUT IF YOU CAN'T GET HOLD OF IT, USE FROZEN INSTEAD. IN THE STATES IT'S CUSTOMARY TO USE AROMATIC OLD BAY SEASONING TO SPICE UP CRAB CAKES AND IT'S NOW WIDELY AVAILABLE ONLINE OR IN SUPERMARKETS AND DELIS IN OTHER COUNTRIES, TOO.

1. Make the cocktail sauce: mix all the ingredients together in a bowl and check the seasoning. Cover and chill in the fridge until ready to serve.
2. In a bowl, mix the mayonnaise, beaten egg, mustard, Worcestershire sauce, lemon juice and Old Bay seasoning (if using). Season with salt and pepper and gently stir in the crab meat, parsley and breadcrumbs – you want the crab meat to stay lumpy and not to flake.
3. Cover and chill in the fridge for 1 hour to firm up.
4. Divide the mixture into 8 portions and shape each one into a patty, about 4cm (1½in) thick.
5. Heat the oil in a large non-stick frying pan (skillet) set over a medium heat. When it's hot, add the crab cakes and cook for 3–4 minutes each side, or until golden brown and crispy.
6. Serve the crab cakes piping hot with the cocktail sauce and lemon wedges for squeezing over.

VARIATIONS
- Use panko breadcrumbs or crushed saltine crackers instead of breadcrumbs.
- Instead of Old Bay seasoning, add a pinch each of sweet or smoked paprika, nutmeg, ginger, celery salt and ground bay leaves.
- Fry in butter instead of oil over a low-medium heat.

REFRIED BEAN TACOS

SERVES 4
PREP 15 MINUTES
COOK 15–20 MINUTES

3 tbsp olive oil
1 red onion, diced
2 garlic cloves, crushed
1 red chilli, diced
2 × 400g (14oz) tins red
   kidney beans, drained
   and rinsed
60ml (2fl oz/¼ cup) chilli or
   hot ketchup, plus extra
   for drizzling
4 spring onions (scallions),
   thinly sliced
8 baby plum tomatoes,
   diced
a handful of coriander
   (cilantro), chopped
8 taco shells
1 small cos (romaine)
   lettuce, shredded
1 avocado, peeled, stoned
   (pitted) and mashed
100g (4oz/1 cup) grated
   Cheddar cheese
salt and freshly ground
   black pepper
soured cream and lime
   wedges, to serve

IF YOU USUALLY BUY REFRIED BEANS IN A TIN, THINK AGAIN AND TRY THIS EASY HOMEMADE VERSION. IT'S SO SIMPLE TO MAKE AND IT'S FLAVOURED WITH YOUR FAVOURITE CONDIMENT – KETCHUP! THIS FILLING ALSO MAKES A DELICIOUS PACKED LUNCH ROLLED UP IN WRAPS OR WHEAT TORTILLAS.

1. Preheat the oven to 180°C (160°C fan)/350°F/gas 4.
2. Heat the olive oil in a frying pan (skillet) set over a low to medium heat and cook the onion, garlic and chilli, stirring occasionally, for 10 minutes, or until the onion is really tender and golden.
3. Stir in the beans and ketchup and heat through gently. Season to taste with salt and pepper. Tip the mixture into a bowl and mash coarsely with a potato masher. Stir in the spring onions, tomatoes and most of the coriander.
4. Meanwhile, place the taco shells on a baking tray (cookie sheet) and heat through in the oven for 4–5 minutes until crisp.
5. Divide the lettuce and refried beans among the taco shells. Top with the mashed avocado and grated cheese, then sprinkle with the remaining coriander. Drizzle with a little more ketchup and serve immediately with soured cream and lime wedges.

VARIATIONS
- **Use black beans instead of kidney.**
- **Add cooked chicken, turkey or chorizo.**

MAIN MEALS

SWEET AND SOUR TOFU

SERVES 4
PREP 20 MINUTES
COOK 15 MINUTES

400g (14oz) extra-firm or
firm tofu
3 tbsp cornflour (cornstarch)
2 tbsp vegetable oil, plus
extra for frying the tofu
2 garlic cloves, crushed
1 green (bell) pepper,
deseeded and cut into
chunks
1 red (bell) pepper, deseeded
and cut into chunks
a bunch of spring onions
(scallions), sliced into
lengths
200g (7oz) mangetout or
sugar snap peas (snow
peas), trimmed
2 fresh or tinned pineapple
rings, cut into chunks
salt and freshly ground
black pepper
cooked brown rice or egg
noodles, to serve

SWEET AND SOUR SAUCE

4 tbsp orange juice
2 tbsp ketchup
2 tbsp soy sauce
1 tbsp sweet chilli sauce
1 tbsp sherry
1 tsp rice vinegar
1 tbsp soft brown sugar
1 tbsp cornflour (cornstarch)

TOFU SERVED IN A SWEET AND SOUR SAUCE WITH BROWN RICE OR NOODLES MAKE A DELICIOUS SUPPER. IT'S QUICK AND EASY TO COOK AND YOU CAN PREPARE THE SAUCE IN ADVANCE.

1. Make the sweet and sour sauce: put all the ingredients in a bowl and stir together until smooth and the cornflour is thoroughly blended.
2. Cut the tofu into 2.5cm (1in) cubes and turn them gently in the cornflour until they are lightly coated all over. Season with salt and pepper and set aside.
3. Heat the oil in a wok or large frying pan (skillet) set over a medium to high heat. When it's hot, add the garlic, peppers, spring onions and mangetout or sugar snaps. Stir-fry for 3–4 minutes, or until just tender but still crisp. Stir in the pineapple and then pour in the sweet and sour sauce.
4. Reduce the heat to medium and keep stirring until the sauce thickens and coats the vegetables. Remove from the heat, cover and keep warm.
5. Pour vegetable oil into a large frying pan until it is about 5mm (¼in) deep and set over a medium heat. When the oil is hot, add the tofu in batches and cook, turning occasionally, for 3–4 minutes until crisp and golden brown. Remove and drain on kitchen paper (paper towels).
6. Stir the tofu into the sweet and sour sauce and warm through gently. Serve immediately with brown rice or egg noodles.

VARIATIONS
- Use fine green beans instead of mangetout or sugar snap peas.
- Add Thai sweet chilli sauce to the sauce.
- Substitute an onion, cut into chunks, for spring onions.

MEXICAN KETCHUP FAJITAS

olive oil, for brushing
2 large red onions, thinly sliced
2 red or green (bell) peppers, deseeded and thinly sliced
4 small lean sirloin or fillet steaks, all visible fat removed
8 flour or corn tortilla wraps
a few crisp cos (romaine) lettuce leaves, shredded
a handful of coriander (cilantro), chopped
8 tbsp grated Cheddar or Monterey Jack cheese
8 tbsp Ketchup Pico de Gallo (see page 14)
salt and freshly ground black pepper
soured cream and Chunky Ketchup Guacamole (see page 23), to serve
lime wedges, for squeezing

WHO DOESN'T LIKE FAJITAS? THEY ARE A GREAT FAMILY SUPPER – QUICK AND EASY AND JUST PUT EVERYTHING ON THE TABLE SO EVERYONE ASSEMBLES THEIR OWN. THE KETCHUP PICO DE GALLO ADDS THE SPECIAL FINISHING TOUCHES TO THIS DELICIOUS MEAL. SERVE WITH MEXICAN BEER OR MARGARITAS.

1. Lightly brush a non-stick ridged griddle pan with oil and place over a medium heat. Add the onions and peppers and cook for 6–8 minutes, turning occasionally, until tender and slightly charred. Remove and keep warm.
2. Increase the heat to high and add the steaks. Cook for 2–4 minutes each side, depending on how rare or well done you like them. Remove from the pan and leave to rest for 5 minutes before cutting into thin slices.
3. Meanwhile, place the tortilla wraps, one at a time, in the hot pan – just long enough to warm them through. (Alternatively, warm them in the microwave.)
4. Top the warm tortillas with the lettuce and coriander. Season lightly with salt and pepper and add the steak strips together with the peppers and onions. Sprinkle with grated cheese and drizzle the ketchup pico de gallo over the top. Roll up the tortillas and eat immediately with soured cream and guacamole, and lime wedges for squeezing.

VARIATIONS
- Use griddled chicken, king prawns (jumbo shrimp) or tofu instead of steak.
- Add griddled courgette (zucchini), spring onions (scallions) or asparagus.
- Cook a sliced hot chilli with the peppers and onions.
- Add diced or sliced avocado to the fajitas.

SERVES 4
PREP 10 MINUTES
COOK 1 HOUR

2 tbsp sunflower or olive oil
2 fat spicy sausages, e.g.
  Toulouse or chorizo,
  thickly sliced
4 chicken thighs (skin on and
  bone in)
1 onion, finely chopped
2 celery sticks, finely
  chopped
2 red or green (bell) peppers,
  deseeded and diced
3 garlic cloves, crushed
1 tbsp sweet paprika
1 tsp cayenne
1 tsp crushed black
  peppercorns
2 sprigs of thyme, leaves
  stripped
2 bay leaves
600ml (1 pint/2½ cups) hot
  chicken stock
1 × 400g (14oz) tin chopped
  tomatoes
3–4 tbsp ketchup
1 tsp Tabasco, plus extra for
  drizzling
350g (12oz/1½ cups) long-
  grain rice (dried weight)
300g (10oz) raw shelled king
  prawns (jumbo shrimp)
juice of 1 lemon
4 spring onions (scallions),
  thinly sliced

JAMBALAYA

THIS HOT AND SPICY CREOLE DISH ORIGINATED IN NEW ORLEANS. IT'S UNUSUAL IN THAT IT COMBINES SURF AND TURF – PRAWNS (SHRIMP), SAUSAGES AND CHICKEN. ADDING KETCHUP MAKES IT EVEN MORE PIQUANT AND COLOURFUL.

1. Pour the oil into a large deep sauté pan or frying pan (skillet) with a lid and set over a medium to high heat. Cook the sausages, turning halfway, for 5 minutes, or until browned, cooked through and the fat starts to run. Remove and drain on kitchen paper (paper towels).
2. Add the chicken thighs to the pan and cook, turning occasionally, for 8–10 minutes until browned all over. Remove and drain on kitchen paper (paper towels).
3. Add the onion, celery, peppers and garlic and cook, stirring occasionally, over a medium heat for 6–8 minutes, or until tender. Stir in the spices, thyme and bay leaves and cook for 1 minute. Add the stock, tomatoes, ketchup and Tabasco and return the chicken to the pan. Simmer gently for 10 minutes, then add the rice. Cover and cook over a very low heat for 15 minutes, or until the rice is tender.
4. Stir in the sausages and prawns and cook gently for 2–3 minutes, or until the prawns turn pink. Turn off the heat and remove the chicken. Cover and leave for 10 minutes.
5. When the chicken is cool enough to handle, strip the meat from the bone and cut into smaller pieces. Return to the jambalaya and stir in the lemon juice. Serve immediately, sprinkled with spring onions and drizzled with Tabasco.

VARIATIONS
- For a really authentic touch, add some okra.
- Add some cooked mussels or clams.
- Add some bacon lardons, pancetta or ham.

GREEK BAKED FISH

450g (1lb) potatoes, peeled and thinly sliced
900g (2lb) thick white fish fillets, e.g. cod, haddock, bream, monkfish (anglerfish)
juice of 1 lemon
3 tbsp olive oil, plus extra for drizzling
4 garlic cloves, crushed
300g (10oz) cherry tomatoes
1 × 400g (14oz) tin chopped tomatoes
2–3 tbsp ketchup
1 tsp dried oregano
1 tsp sugar
12 juicy black olives
a handful of flat-leaf parsley, chopped, plus extra for sprinkling
120ml (4fl oz/½ cup) white wine
salt and freshly ground black pepper

TIP:
This tastes good served lukewarm or even cold.

THIS IS A DELICIOUS AND HEALTHY WAY TO COOK FISH, AND BECAUSE IT IS BAKED IN THE OVEN THERE ARE NO FISHY SMELLS TO LINGER IN THE KITCHEN. NOTHING COULD BE EASIER: YOU JUST PUT EVERYTHING IN ONE DISH AND THEN RELAX WITH YOUR FEET UP UNTIL DINNER IS SERVED.

1. Preheat the oven to 190°C (170°C fan)/375°F/gas 5.
2. Put the sliced potatoes into a large ovenproof dish. Place the fish fillets on top and drizzle with the lemon juice and olive oil. Season with salt and pepper.
3. Mix together the garlic, cherry tomatoes, tinned tomatoes, ketchup, oregano, sugar, olives, parsley and white wine. Pour this over the fish.
4. Cover with foil and bake in the preheated oven for 20 minutes. Remove the foil and bake for a further 20–25 minutes, or until the fish is cooked and flakes easily and the sauce has reduced and thickened.
5. Check the seasoning and then divide between 4 serving plates. Serve, drizzled with olive oil and sprinkled with more parsley.

VARIATIONS
- Substitute red wine for white.
- Add some thinly sliced onion or celery.

SERVES 4
PREP 20 MINUTES
COOK 45–50 MINUTES

a large pinch of salt
1 tsp crushed Szechuan
    peppercorns
2 tsp Chinese five-spice
    powder
½ tsp ground ginger
8 small (or 4 large) free-
    range duck legs, skinned
oil, for brushing
16 Chinese pancakes
½ cucumber, cut into thin
    matchsticks
8 spring onions (scallions),
    shredded lengthways
boiled or steamed rice, to
    serve

HOISIN KETCHUP SAUCE
60ml (2fl oz/¼ cup) ketchup
2 tbsp hoisin sauce
1 tbsp soy sauce
1 tsp clear honey
a dash of lime juice

VARIATIONS
- Substitute plum sauce
  for hoisin sauce.
- Use grated fresh root
  ginger instead of
  ground ginger.
- Use hot ketchup for
  hoisin ketchup sauce.

CRISPY DUCK WITH HOISIN KETCHUP SAUCE

CHINESE CRISPY DUCK IS MUCH EASIER TO MAKE THAN YOU MIGHT THINK. THE HANDS-ON PREPARATION DOESN'T TAKE LONG AND IT COOKS IN LESS THAN AN HOUR IN A HOT OVEN. YOU CAN BUY PACKS OF READY-MADE CHINESE PANCAKES IN MOST BIG SUPERMARKETS, CHINESE FOOD STORES AND ONLINE.

1. Preheat the oven to 200°C (180°C fan)/400°F/gas 6 and line a baking tray (cookie sheet) with foil.
2. Make the hoisin ketchup sauce: mix all the ingredients together in a small bowl. Cover and set aside.
3. In a bowl, mix together the salt, peppercorns, five-spice powder and ginger. Lightly brush the duck legs with oil and then press into the spice mixture until coated all over.
4. Place the duck on the lined baking tray and cook in the preheated oven for 45–50 minutes, or until the meat is thoroughly cooked, browned and crispy on the outside. Using 2 forks, pull the duck meat off the bones and shred it.
5. Meanwhile, warm the pancakes in some foil in a steamer set over a pan of simmering water for a few minutes (or use a microwave). Keep warm in a bamboo steamer basket or cover them with a clean cloth to stop them from drying out.
6. Place the shredded duck on a large serving platter, the cucumber and spring onions on another. Let everyone assemble their pancakes; spread with hoisin ketchup sauce, sprinklewith cucumber and spring onions, and top with duck, then fold or roll up. Serve with rice.

TIP: Use a whole duck; cook at 170°C (150°C fan)/325°F/gas 3 for 2 hours, removing any fat to keep it crispy. Turn up to 200°C (180°C fan)/400°F/gas 6, cook for 15 minutes to crisp it.

SERVES 4
PREP 20 MINUTES
CHILL 30 MINUTES
COOK 25 MINUTES

500g (1lb 2oz/2¼ cups)
   minced (ground) turkey
1 small onion, grated
2 garlic cloves, crushed
grated zest of 1 lemon
a few sprigs of flat-leaf
   parsley, finely chopped
25g (1oz/¼ cup) grated
   Parmesan cheese, plus
   extra to serve
1–2 tbsp olive oil, for frying
400g (14oz) linguine,
   fettuccine or spaghetti
   (dried weight)
salt and freshly ground
   black pepper

TOMATO KETCHUP SAUCE
2 tbsp olive oil
1 onion, diced
3 garlic cloves, crushed
1 × 400g (14oz) tin chopped
   tomatoes
2 tbsp ketchup
1 tsp sugar
a pinch of dried oregano

TURKEY MEATBALLS AND TOMATO KETCHUP SAUCE

THESE MEATBALLS ARE VERY LIGHT AS THEY ARE MADE WITHOUT BREADCRUMBS. CHILLING THEM BEFORE COOKING HELPS TO FIRM THEM UP. IF YOU CAN'T GET TURKEY MINCE, USE CHICKEN INSTEAD.

1. Put the turkey, onion, garlic, lemon zest, parsley and Parmesan in a bowl. Season with salt and pepper and mix together well. Take small handfuls of the mixture in slightly wet hands and squeeze them together to make 16 meatballs. Place on a plate, cover and chill in the fridge for 30 minutes to firm them up.

2. Meanwhile, make the tomato ketchup sauce: heat the oil in a frying pan (skillet) set over a low to medium heat. Add the onion and garlic and cook, stirring occasionally, for 8–10 minutes, until softened but not coloured. Add the tomatoes, ketchup, sugar and oregano and cook for 15 minutes, or until the sauce reduces and thickens. Season to taste with salt and pepper.

3. Heat the oil in a large frying pan set over a medium heat. When hot add the meatballs and cook, turning often, for 10 minutes, or until browned and cooked right through.

4. Meanwhile, cook the pasta according to the packet instructions. Drain and toss with the tomato sauce. Divide between 4 shallow serving dishes and top with the turkey meatballs. Serve immediately, sprinkled with Parmesan.

VARIATIONS
- Add crushed chilli or red pepper flakes to the meatball mixture.
- Use fresh basil or oregano in the ketchup sauce.
- Add a dash of balsamic vinegar to the sauce.

PRAWN PAD THAI

SERVES 4
PREP 10 MINUTES
COOK 8 MINUTES

250g (9oz) flat rice noodles
(dried weight)
2 tbsp groundnut (peanut)
or vegetable oil
4 garlic cloves, crushed
a bunch of spring onions
(scallions), sliced
1 red bird's eye chilli, diced
300g (10oz) raw peeled
prawns (shrimp), cut in
half
3 medium free-range eggs,
lightly beaten
200g (7oz/2 cups)
beansprouts
a handful of coriander
(cilantro), chopped
50g (2oz/scant ½ cup)
crushed roasted peanuts
lime wedges, for squeezing

KETCHUP SAUCE

2 tbsp nam pla (Thai fish
sauce)
2 tbsp ketchup
1 tbsp soy sauce
1 tsp rice vinegar
1 tbsp brown sugar

THIS ZINGY PAD THAI IS SO QUICK TO MAKE AND THE KETCHUP SAUCE GIVES IT A SATISFYINGLY TANGY FLAVOUR. EVEN THOUGH IT MAY SOUND STRANGE, TRY IT AND SEE HOW GOOD IT IS.

1. Prepare the rice noodles according to the instructions on the packet.
2. Make the ketchup sauce: mix together all the ingredients in a small bowl.
3. Heat the oil in a wok or deep frying pan (skillet) set over a high heat. Add the garlic, most of the spring onions and the chilli and stir-fry briskly for 1 minute. Add the prawns and stir-fry for 1–2 minutes, or until they turn pink and are cooked through.
4. Add the rice noodles and stir-fry for 1–2 minutes, then push everything to the side and add the beaten eggs. Cook for 1 minute, stirring until it scrambles. Stir into the noodle mixture and add the beansprouts and ketchup sauce. Stir-fry for 1 minute.
5. Sprinkle with the coriander and divide between 4 shallow serving bowls. Scatter the peanuts and remaining spring onions over the top and serve immediately with lime wedges on the side.

VARIATIONS
- Garnish with a shredded red or green bird's eye chilli.
- Use cubed tofu instead of prawns.
- Add some fresh lime juice and grated zest to the ketchup sauce.

LENTIL SHEPHERD'S PIE

SERVES 4
PREP 25 MINUTES
COOK 1 HOUR

3 tbsp olive oil
1 large onion, chopped
3 garlic cloves, crushed
3 celery sticks, diced
3 large carrots, diced
450g (1lb) mushrooms,
  quartered
1 × 400g (14oz) tin chopped
  tomatoes
3 tbsp ketchup
2 tbsp tomato paste
a pinch of sugar
240ml (8fl oz/1 cup) hot
  vegetable stock
2 × 400g (14oz) tins green
  lentils, rinsed and drained
200g (7oz) baby spinach
  leaves
1 tbsp balsamic vinegar

TOPPING

600g (1lb 5oz) floury
  potatoes, peeled and cut
  into large chunks
400g (14oz) swede
  (rutabaga), peeled and
  cubed
3 tbsp milk (or dairy-free
  nut milk)
3 tbsp olive oil
salt and freshly ground
  black pepper

THIS TASTY PIE, TOPPED WITH MASHED ROOT VEGETABLES, IS A GREAT VEGAN SUPPER. LENTILS ARE PACKED WITH PROTEIN AND DIETARY FIBRE AND ARE VERY SATISFYING AND FILLING. PLUS IT'S A GOOD WAY TO GET YOUR FIVE-A-DAY.

1. Preheat the oven to 200°C (180°C fan)/400°F/gas 6.
2. Heat the oil in a saucepan set over a low heat. Add the onion, garlic, celery and carrots and cook, stirring occasionally, for 10 minutes, or until tender. Stir in the mushrooms and cook for 5 minutes.
3. Add the tomatoes, ketchup, tomato paste, sugar and stock and bring to the boil. Reduce the heat, stir in the lentils and simmer for 15 minutes, or until reduced and thickened. Stir in the spinach and cook for 1 minute until it wilts. Season with salt and pepper and a few drops of balsamic vinegar.
4. Meanwhile, cook the potatoes in a pan of boiling salted water for 15 minutes, or until tender. Cook the swede in a separate pan of boiling salted water for 10–12 minutes, or until tender. Drain both well and mash together coarsely with the milk and olive oil. Season to taste with salt and pepper, and beat until fluffy with a wooden spoon.
5. Transfer the lentil mixture to an ovenproof dish and cover with the mashed potato and swede, right up to the edges. Fluff up the top attractively with a fork.
6. Bake in the preheated oven for 30 minutes until crisp and golden brown on top. Serve immediately.

VARIATIONS

- Substitute tinned beans for the lentils.
- Use a mixture of potatoes and parsnips or sweet potatoes for the topping.
- Spice up the filling with Worcestershire or soy sauce.

3 tbsp olive oil
675g (1½lb) lean stewing beef, cubed and all visible fat removed
2 large onions, chopped
3 carrots, sliced
350g (12oz) swede (rutabaga) or parsnips, peeled and cubed
900g (2lb) potatoes, peeled and cut into chunks
3 celery sticks, thinly sliced
2 garlic cloves, crushed
2 tbsp plain (all-purpose) flour
1.2 litres (2 pints/5 cups) hot beef stock
3 tbsp ketchup
2 tbsp wholegrain mustard
2 bay leaves
1 thin strip orange zest (see Tip)
a small handful of flat-leaf parsley, chopped
salt and freshly ground black pepper
green vegetables, to serve

VARIATIONS
- Use half and half beef stock and red wine.
- Add some bacon or pancetta cubes.

WINTER BEEF AND ROOTS CASEROLE

ON A COLD WINTER'S DAY NOTHING BEATS A WARMING CASSEROLE FOR SUPPER – IT'S THE ULTIMATE COMFORT FOOD. THIS DISH IS PACKED WITH SUCCULENT BEEF AND SATISFYING ROOT VEGETABLES. AND BECAUSE EVERYTHING IS COOKED IN THE SAME DISH, THERE'S MINIMAL WASHING-UP.

1. Preheat the oven to 170°C (150°C fan)/325°F/gas 3.
2. Heat the oil in a large flameproof casserole set over a medium heat. Add the beef and cook for 6–8 minutes, stirring often, until browned all over. Remove with a slotted spoon and set aside on some kitchen paper (paper towels).
3. Add the onions, carrots, swede or parsnips, potatoes, celery and garlic to the casserole. Cook for 6–8 minutes, stirring occasionally, until the vegetables start to soften.
4. Stir in the flour and then gradually add the hot stock, stirring all the time. Bring to the boil and stir in the ketchup and mustard. Return the beef to the casserole with the bay leaves and orange zest. Season lightly with salt and pepper.
5. Cover with a lid and cook in the preheated oven for 1½–2 hours, or until the vegetables are cooked and the beef is really tender. Remove the orange peel and bay leaves and check the seasoning.
6. Serve immediately, sprinkled with parsley, with some green vegetables on the side.

TIP: Use a potato peeler to peel off a long, thin strip of the orange zest without the white pith underneath.

SERVES 4
PREP 15 MINUTES
COOK 25–30 MINUTES

225g (8oz/2¼ cups)
macaroni (dried weight)
1 medium cauliflower,
trimmed and separated
into florets
75g (3oz/scant ½ cup)
butter
50g (2oz/½ cup) plain (all-
purpose) flour
500ml (17fl oz/generous 2
cups) milk
3 tbsp ketchup
200g (7oz/2 cups) grated
Cheddar cheese
150g (5oz) cherry tomatoes,
halved
sea salt and freshly ground
black pepper
cayenne pepper, for dusting

VARIATIONS
- Add some shredded
  spinach or kale.
- Use broccoli instead
  of cauliflower.
- Add some chopped
  parsley to the sauce.
- Add tinned chopped
  tomatoes to the
  sauce.

VEGETARIAN

KETCHUP MAC AND CHEESE

THIS IS COMFORT FOOD AT ITS BEST. ADDING TOMATOES AND CAULIFLOWER TO MACARONI CHEESE TRANSFORMS IT INTO A FILLING SUPPER DISH. WE'VE USED A SHARP CHEDDAR CHEESE BUT YOU COULD SUBSTITUTE GRATED PARMESAN FOR A DELICIOUS ITALIAN FLAVOUR.

1. Preheat the oven to 190°C (170°C fan)/375°F/gas 5.
2. Cook the macaroni according to the instructions on the packet. Drain and set aside.
3. Add the cauliflower to a large saucepan of water and cook for 6–8 minutes, or until just tender but not mushy – the florets should keep their shape. Drain well and pat with kitchen paper (paper towels) to absorb the moisture.
4. Meanwhile, melt the butter in a saucepan set over a low heat. Stir in the flour with a wooden spoon and cook for 2–3 minutes, stirring, until you have a smooth paste. Gradually whisk in the milk, a little at a time, beating until it's all added and free of lumps. Bring to the boil, stirring all the time, until it thickens and you have a smooth, glossy sauce. Reduce the heat to low and cook for 2–3 minutes.
5. Remove the pan from the heat and stir in the ketchup and most of the cheese. Season to taste with salt and pepper.
6. Put the macaroni, cauliflower and tomatoes into a large ovenproof dish and pour the sauce over the top. Sprinkle with the remaining cheese and bake in the preheated oven for 15–20 minutes until piping hot and crisp and golden brown on top. Dust with cayenne pepper and serve immediately.

1 onion, grated
2 garlic cloves, crushed
500g (1lb 2oz/2¼ cups) lean
 minced (ground) beef
1 large free-range egg,
 beaten
50g (2oz/1 cup) fresh
 breadcrumbs
60ml (2fl oz/¼ cup) milk
3 tbsp ketchup
1 tbsp Worcestershire sauce
1 tbsp Dijon mustard
¼ tsp ground paprika
a few sprigs of flat-leaf
 parsley, chopped
salt and freshly ground
 black pepper

KETCHUP GLAZE
120ml (4fl oz/½ cup)
 ketchup
1 tsp red wine vinegar
1 tbsp soft brown sugar
a dash of Tabasco

TIP: You can test whether
the meatloaf is cooked by
inserting a digital instant-
read thermometer – the
internal temperature should
be 70°C (158°F).

KETCHUP MEATLOAF

**THIS CLASSIC MEATLOAF IS TRADITIONALLY SERVED
WITH MASHED POTATOES AND GREEN VEGETABLES –
GOOD OLD–FASHIONED COMFORT FOOD AT ITS BEST. THE
SWEET AND TANGY FLAVOUR OF THE KETCHUP GLAZE
COMPLEMENTS AND ENHANCES THE MEATLOAF, ADDING
THE FINISHING TOUCHES TO A DELICIOUS MEAL.**

1. Preheat the oven to 190°C (170°C fan)/375°F/gas 5 and line
 a 500ml (17fl oz) loaf tin with baking parchment.
2. Make the ketchup glaze: mix all the ingredients together in
 a bowl.
3. Put all the ingredients for the meatloaf in a large bowl and
 mix well until combined. Transfer to the lined loaf tin and
 press down gently, levelling the top.
4. Bake in the preheated oven for 40–45 minutes. Remove
 from the oven and spoon the ketchup glaze over the top.
 Return to the oven and bake for 15–20 minutes, or until the
 meatloaf is cooked through.
5. Remove from the oven and leave to rest in the tin for 10–15
 minutes before cutting into slices to serve.

VARIATIONS
- Use a mixture of minced beef and sausage meat, or
 minced beef and pork.
- Add some grated carrot or shredded spinach leaves.
- Add some garlic powder, onion powder, Italian
 seasoning or horseradish.
- Use natural yoghurt instead of milk.

2 × 1.5kg (3lb) baby back
   pork ribs, each cut into 2
   pieces
2 star anise
1 tsp salt
baked potatoes and salad,
   to serve

BOURBON BBQ GLAZE

120ml (4fl oz/½ cup)
   ketchup
4 tbsp bourbon whiskey
3 tbsp soy sauce
2 tbsp apple cider vinegar
2 tbsp Dijon mustard
a dash of Worcestershire
   sauce
75g (3oz/¾ cup) soft dark
   brown sugar

VARIATIONS

- Add some grated
  fresh root ginger or
  garlic to the glaze.
- Add some chilli sauce
  or a dash of Tabasco.
- Add some ground
  allspice, smoked
  paprika or Chinese
  five-spice powder.

STICKY RIBS WITH BOURBON BBQ GLAZE

THESE GLAZED STICKY RIBS ARE COOKED UNTIL THEY ARE REALLY TENDER AND JUICY. THEY ARE EASY TO PREPARE AND COOK, AND IF YOU DON'T HAVE A BARBECUE YOU CAN FINISH THEM OFF IN THE OVEN AT 200°C (180°C FAN)/400°F/GAS 6 AFTER GLAZING.

1. Preheat the oven to 170°C (150°C fan)/325°F/gas 3.
2. Place the ribs in a large roasting pan and pour boiling water over them – just enough to cover. Add the star anise and salt and cover the pan with foil. Cook for 2–2½ hours, or until the meat is really tender. Remove from the pan.
3. Meanwhile, make the bourbon BBQ glaze: put all the ingredients into a small saucepan set over a low heat and stir until smooth and the sugar has dissolved into the glaze.
4. Heat the barbecue or grill on the medium setting until the flames die down, and the coals are white and really hot. Push the hot coals towards the sides so they won't be directly under the ribs while they are cooking.
5. Brush the glaze over a large sheet of foil and place the ribs on top. Brush more glaze over the ribs and transfer them, still on the sheet of foil, to the barbecue. Cook, basting occasionally, for 10–15 minutes each side, or until they are sticky, shiny, well browned and slightly charred.
6. Separate the ribs and serve immediately with baked potatoes and salad.

INDEX

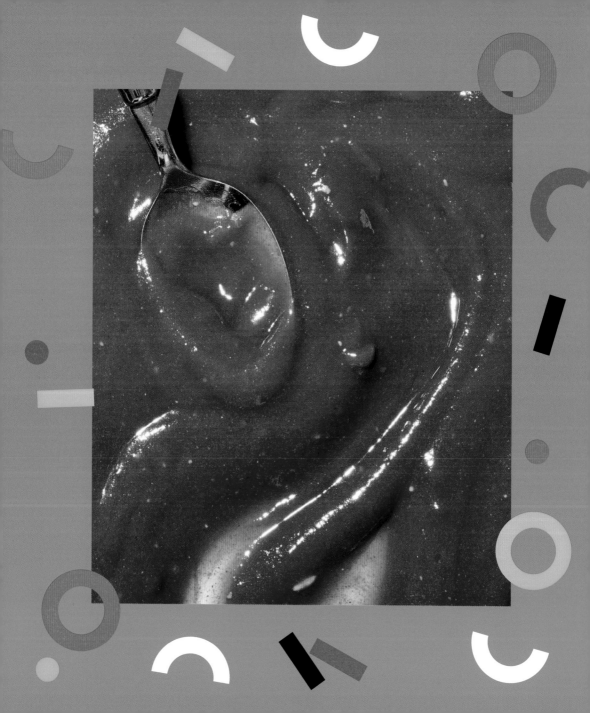